CONFESSIONS
of a Female Pastor
AND OTHER PRAYERS OF THE PEOPLE

JANICE SIX

A NOTE FROM THE PUBLISHER

We try to publish books at TexasStarTrading.com that have strong local community appeal. While Janice's excellent collection of prayers certainly fits that definition, it also should resonate with readers far beyond the boundaries of Abilene, Texas. Sunday school classes, prayer groups, women's conferences all could benefit from Janices's spiritual insights and real-life experiences.

Glenn Dromgoole

© 2023, Janice Six

ISBN: 979-8-9873351-5-4

Published by Texas Star Trading Company

174 Cypress Street, Abilene 70601

www.TexasStarTrading.com

(325) 672-9696

Designed by Tinyah M. Hawkins/Goofidity Designs

Printed in the USA

This book is dedicated to the
church family of

FIRST CENTRAL
PRESBYTERIAN CHURCH,

who has nurtured me in the faith from birth,
and continues to be a source of
inspiration, encouragement, and love.

Contents

PRAYERS OF ADORATION

PRAYERS OF GRATITUDE

Foreword

One of First Central's favorite long-time, all-time members was Dr. B. J. Estes. B. J. always spoke both sincerely and eloquently. I remembered him commenting one day "that Cliff spoke about God, but Janice spoke to God."

That is the truth. Janice's prayers were spoken not to us, but directly to the Lord above. She invited us to pray along with her. As you read this book you will discover a pastor's heart. Janice has a big one.

Missing in this book will be a heartfelt tear or two or three that accompanied the spoken prayer. And then there were the times that Janice prayed with great intensity and conviction. I would sometimes open my eyes and peek ...seeing her hair getting redder and redder! I appreciated her sincere concerns for others who lived both near and far. Janice's heartfelt convictions are easily seen between the lines of these prayers.

I am pleased the book includes some of her benedictions. Here is one of my favorites:

Life is precious;
treasure every moment.
Life is fragile;
handle with prayer.

Life is a gift;

be surprised by joy.

Read these wonderful prayers as you discover them in the context of the real needs of life. I think they will help you to pray your own prayers. As in so many spiritual things, the "ability to pray," especially in times of trouble, is God's gift. But the "resolve to pray" is our calling!

Let us pray......

Cliff Stewart, Senior Pastor
First Central Presbyterian Church
Abilene, Texas

Introduction

I must confess that the idea to write this book was not my own. Church members and friends over the years have been asking me to pull together some of the prayers that I've been led to write and pray during worship services, Wednesday night dinners, Bible studies, and other times when God's people have gathered. I confess that I questioned how seriously to take this request. Would people really be interested in reading a book of prayers? Would it be presumptuous to share my prayers as if anyone needs words other than their own to pray? I'm also aware that there are people who deem spontaneous prayers superior to those written. The thought is that because they are spontaneous, they are more sincere and God-directed than those that may have been written days or even decades earlier. I haven't always found this to be true.

What I do know to be true is that praying with a pen or on a computer helps me pray more earnestly, since committing words to paper allows time for reflection, pondering, and reconsideration. I've also experienced epiphanies during times of prayer—insights and thoughts that seemed to come straight from the One who nudges us to pray. The memory of these special moments continues to offer reassurance of God's presence and participation in prayer—written as well as spontaneous.

In an attempt to make *Confessions of a Female Pastor* more relatable to your own life experiences, I have included stories and scripture passages that lend a context to each of the prayers being shared on these pages. My hope is that this collection will prompt you to reflect on your own journey, and by so doing, you'll recognize, or be reminded, of God's invisible footsteps alongside your own as you continue the journey. I also hope that the next time it occurs to you to pray, you will imagine God tapping you on the shoulder and saying, "Talk to me," and you'll consider this your invitation to pray.

PRAYERS OF CONFESSION

"If we say that we have no sin, we deceive ourselves, and the
truth is not in us.
If we confess our sins, he who is faithful and just will forgive
us our sins and
cleanse us from all unrighteousness."

I JOHN 1:8-9

The Gift of Confession

The first two questions God asked—according to scripture—were of Adam and Eve. The first question: "Where are you?" and the second question: "What have you done?" God knew the answer to both questions before asking them. Nonetheless, both questions were important to ask.

What parent hasn't asked the same two questions, "Where are you?" and "What have you done?" knowing full well the answer to both.

So the question we might pose to God and parents is, "Why ask if you already know the answer?" First, these questions are not in pursuit of information, but of confession. Requiring a child—no matter the age—to verbally acknowledge his or her wrongdoing is the first step toward redemption. Divine and earthly parents, alike, want to make sure we know where we are and what we've done. This is the starting point. This is confession.

Unless we know where we are—whether we are on the path of right living or lost in the weeds—we won't know which way to go to get back into God's good graces. Knowing where we are usually also leads to reflecting on how and when we got there. Both bits of information can prove to be the answer to the second question: "What did you do?"

Adam and Eve were hiding in the garden. Why? Because they had disobeyed God's instruction to not eat from a particular tree in the garden. When we stand in a child's room and ask, "Where are you?" and he or she sheepishly crawls out from under the bed, we can be pretty sure the next question to ask is, "What have you done?"

These aren't bad questions for us to ask ourselves sometimes. "Where am I?" and "What have I done?" When we're on top of the world, the answer to the second question might be a litany of achievements. When we're in the pit, the answer to "What have I done?" could be an innocent, "I don't know," or "nothing," when bad things happen over which we have had no influence or control. But many times, the question elicits confession— acknowledgment and admission—of sin, or accidental wrongdoing. Either way, the next steps are repentance and making amends, and both are action steps.

Together, confession, repentance, and making amends lead to forgiveness and healing. And when we accept that we are forgiven, we experience freedom from the regret, remorse, guilt, and shame that are associated with sin. Yes, confession is good for the soul. Whether Jewish, Orthodox, Roman Catholic, Protestant, or even agnostic, confession is a gift of God for the people of God. May we humbly and graciously accept it.

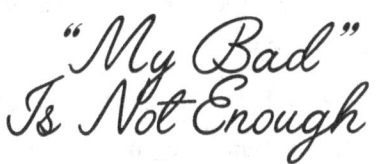

"My Bad" Is Not Enough

Several years ago, when I was teaching high school students, if one of them broke a rule or hurt someone, instead of apologizing by saying "I'm sorry" or "Please forgive me," they would say "My bad." The first time I heard this I wasn't sure what was meant by it. I kept waiting for the person to say more. Simply acknowledging the wrongdoing was just the first step. A time or two I actually said, "Yes, what you did was bad, but what now?" All I got in return was silence and a blank stare. Something is missing when simply acknowledging or confessing the wrongdoing is considered all that's necessary.

Confession is the first step, but repentance is evidence of sincerity. Repentance involves action. It means turning around—heading in a different direction. To feel remorse may prompt us to change our ways, but it is not the change, itself. Repentance requires us to take responsibility for the wrongdoing, and then figure out a way to correct the damage done. Sometimes it isn't possible to repair or replace what's been lost. For example, when trust has been damaged, it takes more than a one-time effort to rebuild it. If confession is as far as we go, odds are we will turn right around and repeat the offense—even if we were sincere when we promised to never do it again. Victims of abuse can testify to this.

Habitual sin has been compared to being on a hamster wheel. Round and round we go. It's a vicious cycle. If we are the least bit accepting of our circumstances and behavior, it's unlikely that we'll make a move to jump from the hamster wheel. However, if our desire for change is intense, and we are willing to take steps to turn and move in a new direction, healing or transformation is possible. William Barclay put it this way, "The power of God never dispenses with human effort...when our will and God's power co-operate, miracles can happen."

PRAYER

Patient and Faithful Lord, we pray for your healing touch upon our lives, yet we fail to do our part to bring it about. We are quick to blame others for our struggles and conveniently ignore our own responsibility for the consequences of our actions. Please forgive us when we choose to languish in situations and conditions by refusing to make necessary changes.

We admit that we can be a stiff-necked people when we stubbornly insist on going our own way rather than looking to you for direction and the strength needed to follow through. We humbly ask for your forgiveness. Please give us the courage to take the next step toward healing and wholeness. Amen.

Forgiving Ourselves

In scripture, there are several examples of people faced with forgiving themselves. King David's story is a good example of how one poor choice leads to another and another. It's like the snowball that grows bigger and bigger as it rolls down the hill and finally hits bottom. Often the damages are irreversible. This was certainly the case with King David.

Power coupled with lust led to sin, resulting in an unplanned pregnancy of another man's wife. This prompts King David to attempt a cover-up. The cover-up is foiled by the honorable husband. Desperate, King David sends word to the husband's commander to place him on the front line—for the expressed purpose of getting him killed. Sadly, the plan works. The man is killed, the wife grieves. King David sends for the woman who is pregnant with his child. He takes her as his wife. The baby dies. King David cries. At this point, King David has not faced his own culpability in all that has happened. It isn't until the prophet Nathan uses a powerful word picture to tap into King David's empathetic emotions that he "comes to himself" and confesses, *"I have sinned against the Lord."* But it's not until we turn to Psalm 51 that we realize the extent of King David's remorse. He writes:

"Have mercy on me, O God, according to your steadfast love; according to your abundant mercy blot out my transgressions. Wash me thoroughly from my iniquity and cleanse me from my sin. For I know my transgressions, and my sin is ever before me. Against you, you alone, have I sinned, and done what is evil in your sight, so that you are justified in your sentence and blameless when you pass judgment."

How do *you* work through *your* regret and guilt? Part of coming to terms with our wrongdoing is counting the cost. Something is always lost, and then there are consequences—not just for the ones we've wronged, but for ourselves. Feelings of remorse, guilt, and shame bore into our hearts and are not easily extracted. When our feelings act as bullies, our soul suffers. We have to face the bullies or they will continue to chase and taunt us. We have to call them by name and turn them over to God, and in God's hands our feelings can be brought under control and be redeemed. Only God has the balm to bring relief.

To forgive or be forgiven does not nullify the consequences or diminish the severity of the wrong action, but forgiveness and transformed living are necessary for hope to be restored.

PRAYER

Merciful God, the sin of my past keeps pounding on the door of tomorrow, threatening to rob it of its beauty and potential. I know the wrong I have done, and the suffering I have caused others. Help me know what to do that can bring healing to those I have injured.

Lord, without your help, I know I will not be able to shake free of the guilt and shame that torments me day and night. I need you, Lord, to quite all voices but your own. I need your peace. Please, Lord, help me forgive myself as you have forgiven me—fully. Amen.

God Bless This Land

July 4th of each year is a day when we celebrate this land of freedom and opportunity. With all the hoopla and hoorays being expressed, it's easy to think of ourselves "more highly than we ought," as Paul warned the Romans. We may forget that in God's perfect world, it's level at the foot of the cross, and we are all standing shoulder-to-shoulder and hand-in-hand.

When God renews the face of the earth, there will be no more greed, and that for which we pray today will be a non-issue.

The following prayer of confession is intended to be read responsively by a community of faith. Of course, it can also be read individually.

PRAYER

In this land of plenty, Lord...

We confess our insatiable appetite as we cry, "More! More!" with our mouths full.

In this land of the free, Lord...

We confess our obsession with control not only of ourselves but over the lives of those with whom we live and even over the choices of strangers whose ways are

not our ways.

In this land of opportunity, Lord...

We confess our sluggishness when it comes to reaching beyond the sure and certain or pulling ourselves up onto our feet to step out on faith.

As a community gathered in your name...

We ask for forgiveness when we have taken for granted the provisions you have poured out upon us, and the opportunities we have ignored to sow the seeds of love, joy, and peace in your name right here in our corner of the world.

Amen.

Wandering Minds

Mindfulness, meditation, breathe prayers, journaling are all practices promoted to silence the "committee" in our heads that seems to constantly be in session.

There's an art to listening, and apparently there is an art to focusing our attention long enough to pray. This is nothing new.

I don't remember consciously deciding to write my prayers, but from a young age that is what I've done. At that time, it was called "keeping a diary." I didn't set out to write a prayer. I was simply writing about the highlights and low points of a day. However, as I wrote, the entry would evolve into prayer. This practice has continued and I'm grateful, for a couple of reasons.

One benefit of praying on paper has been the historical record it provides—providing the prayers are saved. I have prayers written the days leading up to the birth of Greg, our first child, and the same for Julia, our daughter. Until they were mentally mature enough to retain and recall memories, I kept a journal for each. Many entries in these little books are prayers. Now that they are adults, it's been interesting, and often entertaining, to look back at them and note how much of what I prayed either came to pass or, by the grace of God, didn't.

A second benefit I've recognized, especially with the use of a computer, is how praying on my keyboard has often been cathartic. Because I believe all prayer is initiated by God, I actively listen to what I'm being compelled to type. It's been a way of sorting my thoughts, bringing deep-seated feelings to the surface of my consciousness, which often allows me to examine and work through any I wasn't aware of feeling. Problems have been solved, when possible solutions have come to mind, and sometimes I've been convicted of my culpability that has contributed to the problem.

Once I became a pastor, and often responsible for offering the prayers of the people, writing has helped me address the challenge of considering the diversity of concerns on the hearts of the congregation, and also the diversity of the congregation itself. I would often spend at least an hour praying and committing the "long prayer" to paper.

The majority of the prayers in this book have been prayed in worship, and because they were prayed on paper, we can pray them together years later.

PRAYER

Prompted to pray, Lord, we close our eyes, shutting down our sense of sight. For some of us, this tends to give our imaginations permission to wander. Rather than focusing on you, our first thoughts are of ourselves. Instead of being attuned to your still small voice, we allow the incessant chatter that goes on in our head to drown out anything you may be trying to say to us today.

We trust that you know us better than we know ourselves and know our needs before we ask. For these reasons, we have the courage to entrust both our dreams and dreads to your care.

Because we have faith in your goodness, faithfulness, and love, we can honestly pray, "Thy will be done."

In this moment, bless us with an assurance of your presence, Lord. Quiet all voices but your own as we attentively listen and watch for your direction. Amen.

Presbyopia

There is an eye condition that has much in common with our sinfulness. The condition is called Presbyopia, and it is characterized by weakness and loss of elasticity—becoming rigid. This results in difficulty to see what is closest to us. Sinfulness can be described in the same way.

Whether it's an old habit or a skewed belief, both can become so familiar to us that we fail to see them for what they are. "I've always done it this way," or "This is just the way I am" are not valid reasons for maintaining the status quo.

Just because it's always been done one way doesn't assure us that it is right or best. To excuse our poor behavior or prejudicial mindset as acceptable because it's "just the way I am" is to deny God's power and desire to help us change.

In most cases there isn't a desire to change, because there is no recognition that change is needed. The familiar is comfortable. Change feels foreign. Change requires effort. Sometimes we'd rather continue as we are than make a change—even when we know change is needed.

Presbyopia is a condition that obstructs our vision, and the same can be said of sin. People are blinded all the time by sin and a prideful stubbornness to remain the way we are.

PRAYER

God of All, we admit that we're not always comfortable with your generous hospitality and the inclusive nature of Christ. Sometimes we question whether "all" are really your children. We are inclined to make your love conditional, based on what we consider acceptable.

We're so conditioned to compete and achieve that it's hard for us to accept that there is nothing we can do to earn our salvation and nothing we can do that is beyond your will to forgive. Forgive our hesitancy to share your desire that all come to know Jesus as Lord. Amen.

Taking Care of Business

"Give your entire attention to what God is doing right now, and don't get worked up about what may or may not happen tomorrow. God will help you deal with whatever hard things come up when the time comes."
Matthew 6:34 MSG

It was July 6, 2002. It had been raining all week in our West Texas town. The ground was already saturated when four to six more inches were dumped on us in a brief period of time, causing the creeks to break out of their bounds.

More than six hundred homes and fifty-one businesses were flooded. Fifteen of the six-hundred homes belonged to members of our church. One of the homes belonged to our Associate Pastor, and Cliff was out of the country. That meant I would have my hands full for the next three weeks!

To help out I assumed the preaching, and visitation of those in the hospital, and now these fifteen families were added to list. One of the first things I was charged with doing was on behalf of Presbyterian Disaster Assistance, who had immediately cut a check of several hundred dollars for each of the families from our congregation. I was to deliver the checks and assure them that more help would be forthcoming as needed.

One afternoon as I left one member's home my mind was racing, trying to figure out how I was going to get everything done. About that time, these words came to me, "You take care of my business, and I'll take care of you." Almost instantly, any worry that was beginning to mount dissipated. From that day on, I trusted that as long as I was doing what needed to be done for the church, everything else would fall into place. I was right.

I've never been prone to worry, but I have experienced being overwhelmed when I start looking too far down the road, rather than focusing on what's right before me. Those words, "You take care of my business, and I'll take care of you," continue to assure me of God's willingness and power to help me get done what most needs to get done. There's a slogan often quoted in twelve-step programs, "Do the next right thing." It's a reminder to stay in the present and don't let our minds take us too far down the road, where worry awaits.

PRAYER

Steadfast and loving God, we admit that we are an anxious people, and we forfeit the peace you offer through the awareness of your presence. There is much in life we don't understand, Lord, and there are times when we are very impatient as we wait for evidence of you having heard our prayers.

Forgive us when we allow worry to chip away at our hope, as we take the present for granted by fretting over the future. Forgive us for drumming our fingers and devoting more time to worrying than watching for signs of your activity in our lives. Amen.

In Defense of Sin

"Two wrongs don't make a right." How many times have we been scolded using these words, when we attempted to "set the record straight," on our own? Curious as to the origin of this idiom, I discovered that it is thought to have first been cited in the United States in 1783. Supposedly, it was penned in a letter by Dr. Benjamin Rush. Rush was one of the 56 signers of the Declaration of Independence, and a notable physician and educator, living in Philadelphia.

The saying may be attributed to Rush, but the wisdom of its words dates all the way back to Jesus. Speaking to his disciples and the crowd that gathered for what later became known as the Sermon on the Mount, Jesus proclaimed, *"You have heard that it was said, 'An eye for an eye and a tooth for a tooth.' But I say to you, do not resist an evil doer. But if anyone strikes you on the right cheek, turn the other also; and if anyone wants to sue you and take your coat, give your cloak as well; and if anyone forces you to go one mile, go also the second mile..."* (Matthew 5:38- 41)

Expounding on Jesus's teachings, Paul told the Romans, *"Do not repay anyone evil for evil, but take thought for what is noble in the sight of all...Beloved, never avenge yourselves, but leave room for the wrath of God; for it is*

written, 'Vengeance is mine, I will repay, says the Lord.'...
Do not be overcome by evil, but overcome evil with good."
(Romans 12:17-21)

Maybe it has something to do with an innate survival instinct, but most of us—if we don't fight back—at least talk back, which is getting people killed these days. Retaliation is a knee jerk reaction that kicks in when someone wrongs us or someone we love.

Turning the other cheek seems wimpy—certainly not courageous nor noble—making retaliation, and other forms of payback, not only acceptable but applauded by a growing swath of the American population. However, this still doesn't make it right in God's sight.

Martin Luther King, Jr. made an astute observation when he said, "The old law of an eye-for- an-eye leaves everyone blind."

PRAYER

O God, you know us better than we know ourselves. You know our motives, fears, prejudices, and character flaws. Some of us have made an art of rationalizing our wrongdoing. We convince ourselves that our offenses are not that bad, making them that much easier to do the next time. Each time we repeat the offense our conscience is dulled a little more until we eventually find ourselves defending the very sin we once confessed.

Humble our prideful spirit, Lord, so that we may recognize our waywardness, sincerely seek forgiveness and, with your help, repent of the sin that threatens to be our downfall.

Remind us that when we point our finger at our neighbor or our enemy, there are three more pointing back at us. When we are tempted to "take matters into our own hands," temper our human nature to retaliate and remind us to bite our tongue and turn the other cheek—just like Jesus did. Amen.

Short Answers and Clever Comebacks

There's a great deal of chatter about how our attention span is shrinking. Some claim it's now less than a minute, which seems suspicious since Kate Winslet held her breath underwater for more than seven minutes while filming *Avatar: The Way of Water*? Tell me *that* didn't require attention! I'm sure there's research to support the claim but who has the time to check it out?

I don't doubt that our attention is harder to hold than a decade ago. There's just so many more distractions since the door to cyberspace swung open. No way can we keep up! In response, we run faster, cut corners, and reduce the amount of attention we're interested in giving any single activity in our hurried lives. One area of life that suffers is communication.

What we write has been whittled down to phrases and bullet points. Short texts are preferred to emails, and both are favored over handwritten correspondence or even phone calls.

Important decisions are made based on sound bites rather than sound research. Quips and clever answers—whether they are true or not—are at least easy to remember, which makes them more likely to be quoted.

Repeated enough, they are eventually accepted as truth with no further consideration. When it comes to God's word, this is a problem.

I call it sloppy theology. It's when we say things without thoughtful consideration. For example: When Christians say, "Everything happens for a reason," the implication is that whatever happens is God's will. Really? Let's think this through: *Everything*? Does God ordain murders and other violent acts? Are you willing to say that it's God's will when children are sexually abused and exploited? Of course not!

Yes, everything does happen, and many actions are intentional, but it doesn't mean the reasons are ordained by God. There is an obvious answer for why much of what happens in this world cannot be honestly ascribed to God. We call it free will.

Because God chose to give humanity the power to make decisions, and take action without God's approval, bad things happen. Everything may happen for a reason, but the reason might be rooted in greed, jealousy, prejudice, resentment, or a myriad of other hurtful possibilities.

Here's another example of saying what we surely don't believe. A children's book is attempting to offer proof of the extent of God's love for us. Cited was God's choice of parents for each of us. Do you see the problem with this?

The obvious assumption is that we all have loving,

healthy, parents. Sadly, this isn't true. Do we really want young children to equate God's love with their parents' love?

God's love as our heavenly parent far exceeds all the love *any* parents can possibly give their children—even the most conscientious and caring parents. God's love is perfection—the ideal love. *This* is the message our children need to hear, not that their parents' love is an accurate representation of God's love.

Just because a story sounds sweet, or clever words roll off the tongue, doesn't mean they need to be repeated. And just because we've heard an expression all our lives, doesn't make it true. In our haste to get to the point, may we not neglect to seriously consider what we are saying and ascribing to God.

PRAYER

Holy and merciful God, we confess that for the sake of time, we sometimes sacrifice truth. We are tempted to be sloppy with your sacred word by offering short answers based on faulty assumptions and limited perspectives. In our haste or out of laziness, we fail to fully consider what we are saying about you and on your behalf. Awaken us to the power of words and the need to be intentional about what we say—especially when speaking of you. Amen.

None of My Business

We've heard it said that confession is good for the soul, but I say only if confessing will bring healing to the one you've hurt. Let's pretend that a dear friend with whom you've enjoyed many laughs and good times over the years comes to you one day and tells you that for the past two years she's been angry with you. You had no idea!

She goes on to tell you of an incident that is no longer of consequence. At the time, however, for her it sparked all kinds of negative thoughts about you. Now, two years later, she has worked through her negative feelings and wants only for you to forgive her.

Forgive her for what?

Five minutes ago, you never knew there was a problem!

Five minutes ago, there was nothing to forgive.

Then, while you're still reeling from the shock of her confession, she breathes a sigh of relief and says with a broad smile, "I feel so much better now."

You on the other hand, feel lousy and confused. Tell me: who benefited from this confession?

Confessing to the one who never knew and was never hurt by your offense is *not* good for the soul—except for maybe your own. As a wise friend once shared, "Your opinion of me is really none of my business." In this case, I'd say she's right.

PRAYER

God of Grace, may I be as eager to forgive as I am to be forgiven. In my haste to be forgiven, remind me to consider the possible harm that could come from my confession. Give me wisdom to discern the possible consequences—consequences that could harm another.

When it comes to apologizing, may my first concern be for the one I've offended. Remind me that setting things right may take more than a simple, "I'm sorry." Most of all, may my words and actions be sincere. Amen.

PRAYER

Lord, by design you have given us free will and opportunities to exercise it. We confess that we often squander time, choose what benefits us at the expense of others, and more times than not, give little thought to what you would have us do or say. Forgive us, we pray, when we make poor choices that lead us and others astray. Amen.

Jousting with the Lord's Prayer

Imagine, for a moment, attending a funeral for a beloved member of the community. In the congregation are Presbyterians, Baptists, Church of Christ, Methodist, Episcopalians, and many who worship independent of a denomination.

The time comes for the Lord's Prayer to be offered in unison. All heads are bowed, and the prayer begins, "Our Father, who art in heaven, hallowed be Thy name..." Everyone is of one accord. However, midway through the prayer, it's as if the congregation begins speaking in tongues! Some seem to be saying one thing, and others another. They are.

The Presbyterians and Church of Christ are saying "...Forgive us our debts as we forgive our debtors." The Baptists, Catholics, Methodist and Episcopalians are saying, "...Forgive us our trespasses as we forgive those who trespass against us."

It even sounds like the volume has been ratcheted up a decimal or two on this part of the prayer. Could this be a passive aggressive move to drown out the other? I could ask, but how likely is it that anyone is going to confess to jousting with the Lord's Prayer?

You may ask why some denominations and traditions

say "debts" and "debtors," and others say "trespasses" and "those who trespass against us." The answer dates back to 1526 when William Tyndale, a brilliant scholar, credited as one of the first to translate the Bible into English, decided to substitute "trespasses" for "debts" in the Lord's Prayer.

In 1549 Tyndale's version of the Lord's Prayer was adopted by the *Anglican Book of Common Prayer*. This led to its widespread use, and eventually it became the preferred version by many Christians.

The good news is that while Jesus uses "debts" and "debtors" in the prayer, as recorded in Matthew 6:9-13, he goes on to explain what he means by "debts" and "debtors" by using the term "trespasses" in verse 14. Clearly, the two are intended to convey the same message. So, why are we so insistent on using one over the other?

Why not, when worshiping with the Presbyterians, say "debts" and "debtors," and when worshiping with the Methodists, say "trespasses?" From a practical standpoint, this makes sense. Why insist on cramming the 11-syllable phrase into a seven-syllable space, just for the sake of tradition, when the message is the same?

I say we stop jousting with the Lord's Prayer and agree to say "debts" when we're worshiping with debtors, and "trespasses" when we're worshiping with those who trespass against us. It's a small concession for the sake of unity, don't you agree?

PRAYER

God of both debtors and those who trespass against us,

We admit that we are often more devoted to upholding traditions than promoting unity and seeking common ground. From this day on, may we intentionally demonstrate our oneness in Christ by yielding our loyalty to a few words, in order that we may truly pray together in one voice. We ask this in the name of the One who taught us to pray. Amen.

Stack of Bibles

One evening while tucking Julia into bed, Greg, who was about 10 years old, came into her room carrying a stack of Bibles. The stack reached from his knees to his chin. Hunched over and continuing to hold the huge stack steady with his chin, he explained that he had gone through the house and gathered every Bible he could find.

I was so impressed! First, impressed that Greg was so interested in the Bible that he searched the house to find all of them. Second, impressed with how many Bibles we had. Obviously, this was proving to be a positive influence on his growing appreciation of scripture.

Puffed up and beaming with pride, I was silently throwing for myself the mother-of-the-year party when Greg said, "You'd think with all these Bibles in the house, we'd be having a Bible study or something." Ugh!

As quickly as I had soared to cloud nine, I plummeted to the pits. Convicted. My young son made his point: What good does it do to have a stack of Bibles if they stay on the shelf?

PRAYER

Out of the mouths of babes, Lord, we can so quickly be put in our place. Forgive me for apparently placing more value on collecting Bibles than sharing their content with the most impressionable members of our family.

I admit that I have spent more time teaching them camp songs and fairy tales than introducing them to the psalms and stories from scripture. Please forgive me and help me remember the old saying, "What you do speaks so loudly, I can't hear what you're saying." Amen.

God's Dream, But...

One of my favorite children's books is entitled *God's Dream* by Archbishop Desmond TuTu and Douglas Carlton Abrams, illustrated by LeUyen Pham. It opens as a letter, "Dear Child of God..." calling to mind one of the most inclusive and assuring verses in scripture, I John 3:1, *"See what love the Father has lavished on us, that we should be called children of God; and that is what we are..."*

Yes, that is what we are, and that is what *they* are—the stranger from a foreign land, the opponent across the aisle, the bully on the school yard, and all the little children of the world.

Yes, we are all God's children and, according to this book, it is God's dream that all of us share and care for each other. It's God's dream that we hold hands and teach each other our favorite games. It's God's dream that we laugh together and ultimately realize that we are all brothers and sisters to one another.

"But..." This three-letter word is pivotal anytime it is used. In this case, God's dream is one way "but..." But what? But God does not force us to be friends or to love each other. Once again, God loves us enough to take the risk of letting us exercise our freedom to choose who we will love and who we will claim as family. But (here's that word again), it's becoming more and more apparent in this country, that God's dream of a kumbaya society might be considered a nightmare by a growing number of citizens.

In Bill Bishop's book, *The Big Sort: Why the Clustering of Like-Minded America is Tearing Us Apart*, he writes that finding cultural comfort in "people like us" has resulted in the narrowing of communities, political groups, and even churches. He writes, "We have worked quietly and hard to remove any trace of the 'constant clashing of opinions' from daily life." Granted, becoming homogeneous may reduce the tension around the table, but what we stand to lose is an appreciation for accommodating differences through compromise, which is essential to a democratic society that values a shared way of life. If we no longer strive for a shared way of life, God's dream is obviously not our dream. But wait a minute. This is a problem!

If God's dream is unity and love of all people everywhere, then God's will must be the same. This means we, the church, need to wake up and remember that we are often called to be counter to the culture rather than conforming to the ways of the world. We need to also think about what we pray aloud every Sunday morning when we say in unison, "Thy will be done on earth as it is in heaven..." If God's desire is for reconciliation with all creation, we must focus our attention on swinging open the doors of the church for any, and all, to join us for a donut and worship.

Rather than being critical of differences, we need to be applauding the unique perspectives of those who see the world differently than we do. We must make it our aim to work for reconciliation, collaboration, and cooperation in all areas of church life, and resist the temptation to welcome only "people like us." By so doing, we will be striving for God's will to be done on earth as it is in heaven. We will also be helping God's dream come true here and now.

PRAYER

Generous God, we are instructed in scripture to recognize what love you have lavished on us that we should be called your children. We confess that there are some days when we obsess over our own faults to the point of questioning your love for us. There are other days when we can't imagine that your love is inclusive enough to embrace the stranger on the street as one of your children, too. Forgive us for limiting your capacity for love based on our own shallow reservoir. Forgive us when we're more interested in creating the church in our own image than sharing your dream of unity and love with all the children of the world. Amen.

We the Church

I have no words as appropriate and worthy of pondering than those of Paul to the Philippians. Taken to heart, they would not only bring unity to the church but go a long way toward healing this nation and, in turn, the world.

I encourage you to read this passage aloud. These are words that were written to be heard. And as you hear them, listen *for* God's word—not to God's word, but *for* God's message—for the church in this day and time. Trust the Holy Spirit to guide your thoughts and prick your heart.

"If there is any encouragement in Christ, any consolation from love, any sharing in the Spirit, any compassion and sympathy, make my joy complete: be of the same mind, having the same love, being in full accord and of one mind. Do nothing from selfish ambition or conceit, but in humility regard others as better than yourselves. Let each of you look not to your own interest, but to the interests of others.

"Let the same mind be in you that was in Christ Jesus, who, though he was in the form of God, did not regard equality with God as something to be exploited, but emptied himself, taking the form of a slave, being born in human likeness. And being found in human form, he humbled himself and

became obedient to the point of death—even death on a cross."
(Philippians 2:1-8)

This is the word of the Lord...thanks be to God.

PRAYER

Giver of All Life, we the church, stand before you with our heads reverently bowed and with contrite hearts, for like the Israelites, we, too, have lost sight of your overarching will by focusing so intensely on our own welfare and desires. It's obvious, even to us, that Jesus's command to love others as ourselves and his prayer for our unity are as needed today as when he directed them to and about the apostles more than 2000 years ago.

Cocooned in our insulated lives, we confess that we resist sitting with the devastation and grief of those suffering in Haiti or imagining the horror of witnessing the rape of our daughters, the beheading of our husbands or fathers in Afghanistan. Even though we're only a day's drive from the border, we distance ourselves from the plight of the refugees whose hopes of a safe place to raise their children are frayed and unraveling.

Forgive us, Lord, for sinking so deeply into the comforts of our cushy lives that we refuse to simply pray for the suffering, and for those who have heeded your call to be physically present in these places of devastation.

In the days to come, may your Spirit stir the church from placidness, awakening us to meaningful and significant ways we, the church, can respond. Give us the courage necessary to dare ask for our hearts to be broken by that which breaks your heart.

For the sake of an authentic witness to Christ's fortitude, and faithfulness, equip us with foresight, endurance, imagination, and stamina to walk alongside those who are struggling to take the next step without stumbling on this rocky stretch of life's path.

May we, the church, stand united and ready to rise up, and be the church in this fragile and ailing world, and may we do so for your glory. Amen.

Did Jesus Really Have a British Accent?

Why is it that in the 21st century, casting directors and publishers of children's storybooks and other printed material continue to portray Jesus as Anglo-Saxon with chestnut brown hair, fair skin and a British accent? We know from scripture that Jesus was born in a particular geographic region, and that his ministry on earth took place in this same area, so why do we continue to misrepresent his ethnicity? In this age of hyper-sensitivity to misleading stereotypes, and suspicion of motives, it's especially important that the church not be culpable of perpetuating an image of Christ that is blatantly inaccurate.

How much more believable might the good news of Christ's inclusive nature be if his ethnicity were no longer altered for some nebulous reason? I wonder the effect it might have on children, if they were taught from an early age that Jesus was from the Middle East. Would this reduce fear and prejudice against people from the same region? What difference might it make as far as acceptance and respect for people of other ethnicities, if children were exposed to images of Jesus with dark eyes, hair and skin? I wonder if seeing Jesus with dark skin and hair might prove to be affirming to children who share the same. Would children of our church family be surprised to learn that Jesus never spoke English, and certainly didn't have a British accent? If I'm making more of this than is warranted, then why in the first place has Jesus's true ethnicity been ignored all these years? Why do we continue portraying him with chestnut colored hair and white skin?

PRAYER

You hold the whole world in your hands, Lord, yet we are tempted to think of ourselves as favored. Please forgive us for attempting to make you in our own image. Help us to recognize you in the eyes of people we consider different from ourselves, rather than eyeing them with suspicion. Open our minds and hearts to welcome the stranger and be willing to hold hands with your children around the world. Amen.

This is an excerpt from "Did Jesus Really Have a British Accent?" The full essay can be found by visiting Spirit of Abilene: An online faith forum, spiritofabilene.com.

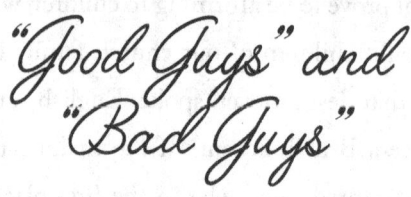

"Good Guys" and "Bad Guys"

It was a simpler time then, back when we watched "Father Knows Best" every afternoon.

Roles were clearly outlined and defined. Men were bread winners and women were bread bakers. Children were to be seen, not heard.

There were the "Haves" and "Have Nots." Most things in life were black or white. There were no shades of gray.

"Sitting on the fence" was viewed as wishy-washy. Everyone chose sides. You were either "in" or "out;" "right or wrong."

There were "good guys" and there were "bad guys." No one could be both.

Times have changed and it's true, few things stay the same. Boundaries are blurred.

Men and women both make and bake the bread these days. Some children are still out of sight, hiding for protection. Other children are virtual, living their lives as characters from another world.

The "Haves" insist on more. The "Have Nots" sigh and settle for less.

Few things in life are considered black or white

anymore. Everything has become some shade of gray. The fence has been torn down, and in its place, a wide wall has been built—wide enough to accommodate the mass majority perched atop it.   All on the wall are watching the two extremes do battle below—like the gladiators of old.

Dare not declare what's "right" and what's "wrong." We've learned that "good guys" make bad choices and "bad guys" aren't all bad.

Here's what I make of all of this: The meaning of words evolves over time and what we think we understand and know to be true may not be at all. For example, a hypocrite in the days of Jesus was just another name for an actor— one who assumed the identity of another. Pretending to be someone he or she was not required the art of character development rather than being considered a character flaw. It was a profession rather than a confession.

Today, to be called "bad" is good! So, when it comes to "good guys" and "bad guys," the "good guys" are still good, but now the "bad guys" are also good—really good. I guess this means "All is good!" or should we say, "All is bad — really bad!"

Jesus warned: *"Do not judge, so that you may not be judged…"* (Matt. 7:1) This sounds like wise advice in today's world.

PRAYER

Patient and Forgiving God, we admit that while we often act and speak with certainty, we may not have a clue what we are saying and doing. Worse than that, we may think we do. Remind us that what we say may not be what others hear. The good we think we're doing may be perceived as selfish and pretentious. Forgive us for being quick to judge others, and slow to see our own faults. May we be humble enough to leave the judging up to you. Amen.

How Long, O Lord?

*On every side the wicked prowl, as vileness is exalted
among humankind…*

*How long, O Lord…How long must I bear pain in my
soul, and have sorrow in my heart all day long?"*

(Psalm 12:8 —13:2)

Headlines, talk radio, newscasts, social media,
conversations over coffee, prayer concerns, everyone
is either fearful or fretful, fed-up, or frustrated. What
is happening to civility? Has suspicion squashed any
assumed innocence of the stranger on the street?

Granted, there is cause for alarm. This headline, "Have
You Seen One of These 33 Missing Texas Children?"
pops up on the screen of my cell phone. I click on it and
immediately it's evident that this isn't an isolated incident.
Google "National Center for Missing and Exploited
Children," to learn more. Nearly thirty children have gone
missing from Cleveland in a two-week period. From New
York to California and all points in between, children are
missing.

There are a number of possible reasons, but the
scariest to me as a grandparent is sexual exploitation of
children and youth. The abduction and coercion of young

people, forcing them into the underworld of human trafficking is an abomination. I know it's nothing new and I know it may be worse in other parts of the world, but is this supposed to make us temper our abhorrence of it? If anything, it's cause for even greater outrage. Isn't there something we can do to put a stop to this abuse?

What tops your list of despicable offenses: Racial profiling, corrupt government, gun violence, road rage, murder? The list goes on. What are we to do? Why isn't more being done? Where do we start? The downward spiral begins with a sense of helplessness that manifests as anger, blame, and frustration. When nothing seems to change, hope starts to subside. It's not long until apathy takes us the rest of the way down. We're done. Stop!

We may give up, but God is faithful. The darker the night sky, the brighter the stars appear to shine. As long as there is life, there is hope.

PRAYER

Night and day, Lord, we cry out for your help and protection. Doomsday predictions are spouted around the clock. Acts of violence are waged against innocent people. We see and listen from a distance, shaking our heads and sometimes our fists. We confess our frustration and inactivity in response to these atrocities. Hiding behind the cross, we admit to only being interested in saving ourselves. Forgive us when we neglect our calling to be agents of reconciliation in our homes, the church, this community, and your world. Forgive us when your young go missing, and our response is to scroll to another story. Amen.

We Don't Know What We Don't Know

We were halfway through the year of perfect vision—2020 and we were astounded by what we had seen and experienced since the last ball dropped in Times Square. In addition to the pandemic, the recently released sequel to the civil rights movement of the '60s had left the nation awash in uncomfortable feelings. We were heartbroken, stunned, perhaps embarrassed, and possibly angry about the turn of events in our country. Some of us had been shocked to learn the degree of systemic racism that had led up to the unleashing of hostility and rage that was sweeping the country, disproving the old adage: "What we don't know won't hurt us." In 2020 we learned: "Oh yes it will!"

The following is my personal confession:

It was late in the afternoon of Thanksgiving Day. My phone rang. It was Sandra, a black woman I had met at Breakfast on Beech Street several years earlier. Sandra was calling from the emergency room, which I had learned wasn't necessarily cause for alarm. Sandra went to the ER for any ache or pain. She had called to see if I would come pick her up and take her home. "Of course," I said. She then added, "And can you give a couple of my friends a ride, too?" Immediately, I was uncomfortable. It was one thing to give Sandra a ride, but I didn't know her friends. I stammered around trying to justify why I wasn't sure, but I'd be there soon to pick her up.

Driving across town, I was feeling so guilty for being hesitant to give her friends a ride. To make myself feel better, I decided to give them money for a cab. However, when I pulled into the drive of the ER, I spotted Sandra and her friends. The apprehension I had been feeling suddenly evaporated. Of course, her friends could have a ride!

Why the instant change of heart? Her friends were white—like me.

Up until that moment I had convinced myself that I wasn't prejudiced. My friendship with Sandra was proof of that—or so I told myself. Yet in that split-second, I came face-to-face with the truth: Somewhere deep inside me there remained an unjustifiable fear of strangers with dark skin. I thought I had left this fear behind with my childhood. I felt so ashamed. I didn't know I had a racist bone in my body until put to the test. On that Thanksgiving afternoon, I regrettable failed the test.

When it comes to systemic racism, I pray for the humility to admit that I may be perpetuating racism without realizing it. I pray, too, for the courage to help uproot deep unintentional racism in myself, the church, and our nation. With head bowed, I pray that Christ will continue to intercede on behalf or myself and others like me, praying, *"Father, forgive them for they know not what they do."* Luke 23:34.

CALL TO CONFESSION

Sometimes the greater sins are not what we do but what we fail to do. And sometimes the most grievous sins we commit are those of which we are unaware.

PRAYER

Merciful God, it's disturbing to think of the number of times we have disappointed you without realizing it. It's even more disturbing to consider how blind we can be to our own wrongdoing. We pray that Jesus's plea from the cross also applies to us: "Father, forgive them for they know not what they do." Amen.

Crisis Christianity

Caught in the storms of life, rash promises are often made. Bargaining with God is what we call it, and it may sound something like this, "Lord, if you're really here..." or, "Jesus if you hear me..." followed by, "Please, oh please get me out of this mess—this storm- and I'll be forever faithful."

Low and behold, the storm passes and you're still standing! The Lord has come through for you! Your cup overflows with gratitude. And for a while you're volunteering for worthwhile causes. You're on your knees every night and in your pew every Sunday. Faithfully, you are orienting your life around Christ. However, as time passes, your enthusiasm for keeping your sights set on things above wanes.

Your attention drifts to other endeavors or maybe back to old ways of doing life—nothing "bad" just wasting time on trivial pursuits, like binge watching your favorite Netflix series, playing some game like Water Sort Puzzle on your phone, or surfing the web in the wee hours of the morning. As I said, nothing bad, just nothing of value. Like empty calories, after a steady diet of consuming nothing but sugar and fat, it starts to show—on the scales and in our daily lifestyle. When called to our attention, we realize we've sunk pretty low. Odds are it'll take another crisis to jar us from the recliner and bring us to our knees and in the pew on Sunday. Once again, the cycle begins. I call this Crisis Christianity.

Crisis Christianity is when our faith and faithfulness swell during a crisis. Our prayer life increases tenfold. We are sincerely grateful, and we absolutely intend to reorient our lives to revolve around Christ, but once the crisis is over or the storm subsides, we drift back into our old ways until the next crisis. Are we so fickle, easily blown one direction and then the other? Is God offended by our Crisis Christian mode? What does it take to maintain a fervent faith?

PRAYER

Faithful and Patient God,

In times of crisis, we cry out to you, "Lord, save us!" and then it's not long after the storm has passed, we look down and see our broken promises scattered on the ground. The intentionality with which we promised to live, with you being central to every decision, and the focus of all our praise, seems to have been nothing more than words written in the sand—words that disappear with the tide. Realizing we have drifted back to our old ways we are embarrassed and frustrated to have broken our promises once again. We admit, Lord, that we are Crisis Christians.

You, however, remain faithful to your word. You, Lord, continue to be with us to the end. Like a loyal parent or best friend, you patiently stand by, ready to listen as we pray, catch us when we fall, and comfort us when we fail. O' that we could be as faithful to you as you are to us! With humility, we ask for your forgiveness. Amen.

Poverty of Spirit

I must confess that my enthusiasm and Christmas joy goes beyond the manger and directly to the mall. I love purchasing, wrapping, and giving gifts. I especially enjoy decorating our home and having parties. Singing Christmas carols, baking cookies and making candy. Even though I have a collection of nativity scenes scattered around the house, it's still so easy to get caught up in all the festivities and lose sight of the miraculous birth of Jesus.

Every year on the first Sunday of Advent, I vow to engage in a daily devotional centered on the coming of the Christ child and every Christmas Eve, I confess my poverty of spirit that allowed me to be so easily lured from the path leading to Bethlehem.

Maybe this year will be different. Maybe this year I'll remember that the gifts that last are those that involve making a treasured memory. Maybe this year I'll remember that there are people who dread the holidays because their deficiencies are more pronounced. Their lives do not resemble the Hallmark Christmas cards with family and friends gathered around, sharing gifts, enjoying a feast, and filling their homes with laughter. This year, may we make it our aim to shine the Light of Christ in darkest corners of our communities.

PRAYER

This time of year, Lord, our poverty of Spirit is brought to light, when that for which we yearn has little or nothing to do with you, and everything to do with ourselves.

Amid all that sparkles and glows, we admit that we're more at home in a mall than in a sanctuary. Forgive us, we pray, when we're more likely to reach for Elf on the Shelf than your Word that shares the same space.

O' Lord, how far have we strayed from your intent for our celebration of your Son's birth? Guide us onto the path that leads to the manger. Amen.

Questioning Faith

Every prayer I've prayed for more than a decade have included a couple of the same requests—over and over. I know God hears me. I've never doubted this. I guess this is why I didn't give up several years ago when it seemed that nothing was happening. However, I never considered dropping the request and giving up. Never.

Nonetheless, there was one day when I was feeling particularly anxious about the situation. During the prayer, as I began prescribing what I thought would be best, it was as if God interrupted and with strength and clarity said, "I've got this."

Suddenly, the anxiety I had been experiencing was transformed into peace. I remember breathing a sigh of relief and the tone of my prayer immediately turned to thanksgiving.

From that time on for the next few years. anytime I would begin to wonder, "How long, Lord, how long?" I would hear those words of assurance, "I've got this," and once again, I would draw a breath of relief, and my faith would be bolstered.

PRAYER

Dear God, can it be that you have answered my prayer? There's a part of me that is hesitant to fully embrace what is finally before me. Is it a lack of faith that's pushing down a zealous enthusiasm I long to unleash, or caution that comes with having been unknowingly wrong for so long?

The lack of faith is not in you, Lord. No, you are my refuge and strength. I cherish the faith you have given me to hold fast to your promises and trust in your faithfulness. The lack of faith is in my ability to discern what is true. For so long, I have honestly believed my perceptions to be trustworthy. Now, I hesitate.

The picture I've painted of life has been true only in my mind's eye. I've been blind to fledgling difficulties, unwittingly choosing to ignore a red flag or two I saw along the way. I've favored an illusion of well-being to protect my pleasing perceptions. Without realizing it, I have favored peace at the expense of truth.

So, here I am, Lord, eager to celebrate what I think I see, but hesitant to trust my ability to discern what is real from what I hope it to be. What if I'm still misreading reality to suit myself? Help me, Lord, to know what is true and give me the courage to embrace the fullness of life in this very moment. Amen.

Sing!

When caught in life's storms, sing!

According to the Sing Up Foundation and numerous studies on the effects of singing on the brain, singing lowers cortisol and relieves stress and tension. It also releases endorphins and a hormone called Oxytocin, which results in a flow of positive feelings, increased energy and enhanced feelings of trust and bonding. Granted, singing will not calm the storms that threaten us, but it certainly may calm us in the midst of the storm, especially if the songs we are singing undergird our faith.

From the time I was a young girl, I have enjoyed singing hymns on sunny days for enjoyment and dark days for encouragement. I have literally sung myself and my children through a torrential rain by singing "How Great Thou Art." Often while praying, a song will come to mind, and I'll begin to sing. "When Peace Like a River," often referred to as "It Is Well with My Soul," is a favorite. It was written in 1876 by Horatio G. Spafford after he learned that his four daughters had died in a tragic shipwreck. The circumstances under which it was written, along with the words, are a testimony to the buoyancy of faith.

Recently, I began singing a new song. It's one I learned from my four-year-old granddaughter,

Greer Louise, who brought home a CD she was given at VBS. The first time I heard it, I cried and vowed that I would learn it by heart. The song, published by Group Publishing, is entitled "Never Let Go of Me." For added emphasis, I made up hand motions for the chorus. The physical expression seems to address my need to "Do something!" during times when everything is out of my control. The chorus repeats over and over for three or four times. With each refrain my conviction grows stronger: Yes, God *will* see us through every storm of life.

PRAYER

In times like these, Lord, you call us to anchor deep but that requires staying in the boat, confronting the storm as we move away from the familiar into uncharted waters. We confess that it's tempting to want to remain on dry land, ignoring the imminent dangers of the status quo. Just as in the beginning your Spirit moved over the waters, calming the chaos, we pray for your Spirit to move over us and bring us peace in times of trouble. Amen.

Independence

I came of age in the '70s singing loud and strong with Helen Reddy's hit single "I Am Woman." I was a loyal fan of female singer songwriters like Joni Mitchell, Janis Ian, Carly Simon, and Carole King. I traded my subscription to *Seventeen* for *Cosmo* (short for *Cosmopolitan*) *Magazine* when I went off to college, where I first experienced a sense of independence. I realized that for the first time in my life I could go and do whatever I wanted, and no one would know—"no one" being my parents.

Back in the day, my favorite tee shirt was a promotion for Virginia Slims, even though I never smoked. I bought it because it celebrated Billie Jean King having beaten Bobby Riggs on the tennis court in what was dubbed the "Battle of the Sexes." It read, "You've come a long way, baby."

During my senior year of college, I was asked to write a weekly column for the campus newspaper with the freedom to write about anything I wanted, so I did. This led to one of my favorite compliments. It came from a freshman guy, who declared, "You're the Barbara Walters of Tarleton!" I had arrived!

I was now an adult with a full-time professional career in a faraway land—the Rio Grande Valley. Living alone, and knowing no one other than my co-workers, it was the first time in my life I dreaded the weekends. To fill my time, I decided to launch a self-improvement campaign, which consisted of jogging through a nearby orange grove and eating a cup of yogurt for dinner every evening. I also made it my mission to continue doing things I enjoyed by learning how to comfortably do them alone, like going to the movie and eating in restaurants.

As it turned out, learning to take myself to the movies, and working up to being able to dine in a sit-down restaurant without having a book to read, proved invaluable in my next career that required me to travel several days each week—alone most of the time.

I also adopted a theme song, "Best Friend" by Helen Reddy, and I sang it at least once a day. It was like having my own personal pep rally! The lyrics encourage being as good to yourself as you would be to a best friend. The song ends on a high note with these words, "I'm as nice to me as anyone I know." Perfect! Especially when you're the *only* one you know.

All this to say, I know how to be independent. I used to be *so* independent that I'd tackle group projects on my own—alone. This isn't good. What I eventually realized was that when I did this, I was robbing myself of the opportunity to work alongside some wonderful people. I also came to see that going it alone could be interpreted as having a lack of confidence in others, who, like me, were eager to engage in worthwhile, purposeful work.

I know as Americans, we pride ourselves in being independent and self-sufficient, but it's not always best. Apparently, Jesus knew this. Instead of going solo, Jesus gathered a small community to join him in his work. There's much to be said for *interdependence* and collaboration. Perhaps these are two words we need to put into practice and a mindset worth adopting.

PRAYER

Great Three in One, even though we know that Jesus surrounded himself with a group of twelve, we often consider ourselves weak when we're unable to make it on our own. We deceive and defeat ourselves when we make self-sufficiency our goal and independence a virtue.

Please forgive us for allowing our stubborn pride to shove people away when we need them most. Prompt us to remember that we are created to be in community. We are created to be members of the body of Christ. Give us the humility to accept that we are stronger and better together than apart. Amen.

Lone Ranger Christians

Years ago, I began hearing pastors say, "There are no Lone Ranger Christians." Today there is a growing number of believers who would argue this claim. These are Christians who often describe themselves as "spiritual but not religious," which usually means they believe in Christ but have no use for the organized church. We could say, they have saddled their horses and ridden away.

Regrettably, some have been hurt and abused by congregations or denominations within the household of faith. They have been shamed and told they don't belong. They are told that they are not wanted nor worthy to be members of God's household. This is not true! Sadly, the damage has been done.

How disturbing it is to imagine the body of Christ being dismembered each time a Christian chooses to walk away. Even more offensive is the image of those who elect to cut themselves off—voluntarily amputating themselves from the body of Christ!

No question, the body of Christ is suffering. Maimed and limping, the church continues to meet together for worship and serve when needs arise. Thankfully, other parts of the body in faraway lands are thriving, but we know that when one part suffers, we all suffer.

Will the church survive? Absolutely! Jesus warned the disciples of the persecution they would face because of him. He also prayed for the unity within the church, knowing that there would be differences of opinion, power struggles, jealousy among brothers and sisters, and misunderstandings. Yet, Jesus made it clear in bold terms that the church would survive, when he told Peter, *"...on this rock I will build my church, and the gates of Hades will not prevail against it."* Matthew 16:18

PRAYER

Loving God, by your grace extended to us through Jesus Christ, you call us to be as one—to be family—yet we resist the unity you desire for us.

Rather than focusing on what unites us, we are quick to notice our differences.

Rather than being eager to hold hands and help each other up when one falls, we are more prone to engage in sibling rivalry. Forgive us when we think of ourselves more highly than we ought, and pridefully turn our backs on each other when we disagree.

Call us to attention, Lord, when we choose to go toe-to-toe with those we oppose within your household, risking the reputation of the church, and reinforcing the prejudice of those who choose to remain outside the threshold of Christ's church.

Forgive us for any judgmental attitudes we have conveyed that may have hurt your children, prompting them to turn away from the family of faith.

Stir within Lone Ranger Christians a yearning to return and a willingness to forgive those who have offended them.

Give those of us in the church the humility to listen to their grievances and the courage to make amends. Tell them, Lord, that we miss them. Amen.

PRAYERS OF ADORATION

"On the glorious splendor of your majesty, and on your wondrous works, I will meditate.
The might of your awesome deeds shall be proclaimed, and I will declare your greatness.
They shall celebrate the fame of your abundant goodness, and shall sing aloud of your righteousness."

PSALM 145:4-7

The Challenge of Adoration

Pure adoration requires intentionality. Because of its nature, as the prayer continues, it either leads to making requests on behalf of others or oneself, or it turns to thanksgiving—not that this wrong. It simply means that it can be a challenge to maintain a state of adoration.

Adoration naturally gives way to gratitude, and in turn, gratitude results in prayers of thanksgiving. However, there is value in the discipline of focusing on adoration in prayer. One reason is that adoration has no room for ego, making it a discipline of humility. Adoration shifts the focus off us and shines the spotlight on the one we adore.

Every aspect of life is enhanced the more time we devote to adoration of the Creator. As we affirm the grandeur of God by praising and proclaiming the attributes of God, faith is nourished and hope revived. We are reminded that God is greater than we are—and this is assuring.

In the Westminster Catechism we declare the primary purpose—chief end—of humanity is to glorify God and enjoy God forever. Thankfully, glorifying God is not restricted to prayer. However, prayers of adoration are one way we are reminded of the magnificence of our maker.

Adoration often leads to making requests of God, since in the act of adoring God, we are reminded of God's power to intervene, heal, prompt, and reveal insights that are lifegiving. Again, both faith and hope are nurtured when we engage in adoration of God, so it's no surprise that requests are forthcoming.

I hope that you will be inspired and challenged to make prayers of adoration an intentional addition to your prayer life if they aren't already. There's a reason that the Prayer of Adoration is the first prayer in a worship service.

Alleluia, Alleluia, Alleluia, Amen!

Easter morning is the high point of the Christian year and stands in stark contrast to the forty days of reflection, regret and remorse, repentance and lament leading up to it.

The following call-and-response prayer invites the body of Christ to audibly participate in an expression of adoration on this day marking the fulfillment of centuries of prophecy and the revelation of the promised Messiah.

PRAYER

King Jesus,

Lord of Lords,

Because you have risen,

We have hope.

Because you live,

We have confidence.

Because you love,

We fall to our knees out of gratitude.

Because you are with us,

We are at peace and live with joy.

Because of you, we gather to worship, proclaim your name,

and sing your praises.
Alleluia,
Alleluia,
Alleluia Amen!

Genesis 1 Woman

Genesis 1 – 2:4

Choose for yourself the creation story you prefer. As for me, I'm a Genesis 1woman and here's why:

From the time I was a young child and probably long before that, the two creation narratives have been harmonized into one. Genesis 1 takes the lead for the first 25 verses, stopping short of the creation of humanity. Here we jump over to Genesis 2 and grab verse 7 that talks about God creating man, then we skip the next seven verses and pick back up with verse 15, wherein God places the man in the garden to care for it. It's during this time that God notices that it's not good for man to be alone, so God creates animals and birds. Interesting. God's first choice for a partner to serve as a helper isn't another person but a menagerie of animals and fowl. No surprise, a suitable partner could not be found. That's when God goes to plan B.

God causes a deep sleep to come over the man during which time God takes a rib from the man's side and from it creates a woman—voila! What's wrong with this picture? Plenty, but let's not debate that right now. Let's rewind to the Genesis 1 account of creation and keep it simple.

Rather than omitting the verses that have to do with how woman came to be, let's see what it says beginning with verse 26: *"Then God said, 'Let us make humankind in our image, according to our likeness..."* The verse goes on to say that God gives both man and woman dominion over all the creatures of the earth, sky, and sea. In verse 27 we read, *"So God created humankind in his image, in the image of God he created them; male and female he created them."*

God created *them.* Three times in this one verse what's stressed is that God created *them.* That means it's a big deal. *Them,* not him. God created *them.* From this point on through the first four verses of chapter 2, all instruction, gifts, responsibility, and authority are given to them. *Them,* not him.

Smoothly and without a single jump, Genesis 1 lays out the entire creation story from day one to day seven. So, what in the world—at least on God's green earth—is the justification for omitting the creation of humanity as recorded in Genesis 1? Does the creation of humanity in Genesis 2 make more sense, thus making it easier for young children to believe? You decide:

Genesis 1: Male and female are created together in God's image.

Genesis 2: Male is created, becomes tired and lonely, God puts him to sleep, removes a rib from his side, fashions it into a woman and gives it back to him as one would any other possession.

As I've already stated, I'm a Genesis 1 woman and that's the story I will share with the little children in my life.

PRAYER

God of All Creation, with a word you broke through the darkness and there was light.

You spoke and the sky and land were each allotted expansive space.

By your word the waters parted, dry land appeared, and the dome overhead was set ablaze with a sun, a moon, and sprinkles of light.

By your design the sky, earth, and from the depths of the sea, life sprang forth at your command.

Then out of your goodness you created both male and female in your image, blessing them with purpose, empowering them with intellect, and granting them both compassion and a creative spirit.

Almighty and loving God, may all that has life and breath, praise your holy name! Amen.

Spontaneous Worship

Spontaneous worship is a term I coined a few years ago while working on a project for my Doctor of Ministry degree. The project was titled, *"The Church as Family Worshipping in Unconventional Settings."* As the term implies, spontaneous worship occurs with little or no forethought and is characterized by a sense of wonder and awe. Unlike most worship services, spontaneous worship requires a willingness to be interrupted, as was the case one Sunday afternoon at the Buffalo Gap Cemetery.

The group of families with young children, who were participating in the project, had agreed to meet me just outside of town at a small country cemetery. The topic for the day was death and eternal life—a rather heavy topic for the preschool crowd, but one about which they often ask many questions, and express much interest.

After having meandered through the cemetery with the preschool children and their parents, we gathered near a small rock chapel to visit about their observations and see what the young ones knew about death and eternal life.

As I was attempting to explain death and eternal life in terms a four-year-old might possibly grasp, I noticed a few of the children huddled around another child, who was apparently holding something in her cupped hands. The children were mesmerized. Stepping closer to see what she was holding, I saw, cradled in the palm of her hands, a small dusty gray bug, commonly referred to as a "roly-poly." The children were amazed as the little bug turned into a ball, right before their eyes!

Since the tiny creature had captured the attention of about a third of the children, it seemed best to abandon the prepared discussion and have the group shift its attention to what was of greater interest to this little crowd: a roly-poly bug.

As children began wondering aloud how they might prompt the little ball of a bug to unroll, it occurred to me how this fascination with one of God's tiny creatures might serve as a springboard for worship.

Speaking softly, I began sharing that God was the creator of all living animals, including bugs. Examining our little specimen, we marveled at God's attention to details, such as the tiny legs—all evenly spaced and in two straight lines. We talked about how the outside of the bug's body was hard, yet it was still flexible enough to roll-up into a ball. Curiosity was giving way to wonder and awe, resulting in a moment ripe for worship!

The more we gazed at the roly-poly, the more we were amazed by God's love to create and care for every little creature on this earth! With our eyes open, we noted the beauty of God's creation, while everyone was encouraged to voice aloud something they saw that God had created, or something they thought was interesting or beautiful. We marveled at how wonderfully made all God's creatures are—even the little roly-poly bug— and we ended our time by giving thanks for the gift of life—all life, and the promise of eternal life, our "forever home" with God.

That Sunday afternoon, for a few minutes, we had sensed the sacredness of sharing an unexpected time of worship, partially led by one of God's smallest creatures, in the middle of a small country cemetery.

PRAYER

Creator God, in life and in death, we belong to you.

Into your household, Jesus has invited us, and it is here we will forever be.

You've blessed us with this world, a beautiful playground, teeming with life.

We are filled with wonder and awe, joy and gratitude. Thank you! Thank you!

And all your children, young and old, shout, "Amen, Alleluia, Amen!"

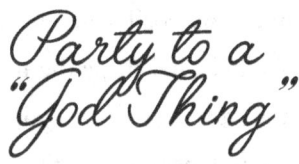

Party to a "God Thing"

Have you ever been a party to a "God thing"—probably without realizing it at the time—but on hindsight, you can see that you contributed to something much bigger than yourself — more significant than you ever imagined.

A "God thing" is the term I use for any event or incident that is unlikely to have taken place or unfolded as it did without God's intervention. Some people chalk these happenings up to coincidence or refer to them as being serendipitous.

Grand Canyon is an entire movie based on such happenings. It's a dramatic portrayal of how intertwined our lives really are—and not just with people we know. In the movie, total strangers become major players in the lives of Mack, played by Kevin Kline, and his wife Claire, played by Mary McDonnell.

There's a scene in the movie where Mack recalls standing on the curb of a busy intersection in Los Angeles. Absorbed in thought, he steps into the street without thinking. Immediately, someone from behind grabs him by the collar and jerks him back—just in time to avoid being run over by a bus. The woman, who was wearing a Pittsburg Pirates baseball cap—his favorite team—literally saved his life! Shaken by the near miss, he looks around to find the woman and she's gone. Maybe she was an angel! Angel or not, people of faith would at least agree that she was a sure sign of God's active presence at work behind the scenes. Some might say it was a "God thing" that she was there at that precise moment and had the wherewithal to jerk him to safety.

It's the helicopter that has captured and held my attention for several years. At various times during the movie, it flies over for no apparent reason. No attention is drawn to it, and it's never mentioned, but it's there. About the third time I saw it, I began to watch for it.

That's how it is with God. Once you recognize God's fingerprints on situations, you begin watching for them. When something occurs that requires an unlikely alignment of events, we call it a "God thing." When something is declared a "God thing," it simply acknowledges a realization that God has been present all along. It's most exciting when we discover that God has been working through us and we had no idea! We've been a party to a "God thing!"

Over time, these "God things" accumulate and it becomes evident that there are no restricted areas –no off-limits—where God cannot be at work. All the world is holy ground, and every situation is ripe with potential and possibilities for God's presence to be made known.

For some, a "God thing" is another word for a miracle. Others reserve the use of the word "miracle" for the supernatural. However, by definition, a miracle is an event that is or appears contrary to what is currently known of nature. I was told once that it's not the event itself that's the miracle. The miracle is the revelation—the "aha" moment, that results from the event. In my book, "God thing" covers both.

I suspect "God things" happens more often than we realize. However, only those with eyes to see recognize God's handiwork. Who knows, you may be a party to a "God thing" right now, and not even know it.

PRAYER

O God, we are eager to recognize your fingerprints on the events of our lives—so eager that we may credit you with more than you have actually done. Others may chastise us for thanking you for a prime parking place or crediting you with running into a friend while vacationing on the other side of the world. Are we wrong to claim these events as "God things?" Are you offended when we see you in all the good that comes our way? Who's to say we're wrong? As long as we're sincere, God, what's the harm in thanking you in all circumstances? Amen.

A Chair for Everyone

It was football season, and the year was 2002. Greg was in high school, and one Saturday afternoon he and some of the neighborhood guys were playing football in the street. One of the guys had brought along his five-year-old brother, who was sitting on the curb watching the "big boys" play ball. Gene had been working in the yard and was aware of the fun everyone was having. This is when he suggested that we see if they'd like to stay for dinner. If so, he'd throw some meat on the grill. What were the odds that a group of high school guys would turn down a homecooked meal? Of course, they accepted!

Gene and I went to work—he at the grill and I in the kitchen. Once the meal was ready, and the table set, we rang the dinner bell! As the guys burst through the front door, they spotted the table and stopped in their tracks. Interestingly, rather than commenting first on the abundance of food, several were most taken back to see the table set with real dishes and cloth napkins. I heard one of the guys ask, "Is this some kind of a holiday?"

After washing up, all took their place around the table. I had set an extra chair at the end of the table beside me, for the little brother. After joining hands for a prayer, the guys "dug in," as my mother used to say.

The memory of this meal, and the look on those guys faces as they tumbled through the front door and saw the table, is one I continue to enjoy. However, the best memory came about a week later, when I was in the grocery store and ran into the mother of the five-year-old boy.

After thanking me for inviting the guys for dinner, she shared what her five-year-old had to say. Instead of commenting on the food, he told her, "Mom, everybody had a chair.'"

Everybody had a chair. Who would have imagined that a five-year-old little boy would have been most impressed simply by having his own chair—his place at the table?

Upon reflection, my thoughts turned to the Messianic banquet, where all will have a place at the Lord's table—young and old alike. No one will be relegated to the "kid's table." We'll all get to sit at the "big table," and Christ will be the host! What a day of rejoicing this will be!

PRAYER

Lord of All, you welcome us into your household with open arms! Your table overflows with the finest of food. Every cup is filled to the brim. You say to one and all, "Come!"

There is no longer a hierarchy of greatness. Those once considered the "least of these" on earth are equal in your sight to those once considered great and powerful in the eyes of the world.

Your table is immense, Lord, and I imagine it to be round by design. You, Lord, are seated in the center—equal distance from each, and every guest. Only you hold a place of honor. Your favor is poured out in equal measure on all who accept your invitation.

What a day of rejoicing it will be when all shall come from east and west, north and south, and take their place at your table! Amen.

Morning, Noon, and Night

See what love the Father has given us, that we should be called children of God; and that is what we are. The reason the world does not know us is that it did not know him. Beloved, we are God's children now; what we will be, has not yet been revealed..." (I John 3:1-2)

PRAYER

Loving and Gracious Heavenly Father, we are humbled by the love you lavish on us— creating and claiming us as your very own through Jesus the Christ. Choosing to call us your children, you welcome us into your household where we have a forever family and forever home. What are we to say? What are we to do but worship you morning, noon, and night!

Rubbing the sleep from our eyes, the events of today have not yet been revealed. New light will be cast on the carryover concerns of yesterday. Our concern is not for the future, but holding fast to the belief that, with you, all is possible. Trusting in your goodness and faithfulness, dawn gives rise to wonder, and joy truly does come with the morning!

As the clock strikes twelve, the day is in full swing. There's still time and a full measure of potential to make this a day to remember. You, Lord, have set us on the path of right living. Your Spirit has come alongside us to coach and, as necessary, coax us through the day. You are the source of all life—the imagination that fuels enthusiasm. And it is enthusiasm that powers our drive to not simply survive but to thrive. You are the compassion that draws us out of ourselves and prompts us to lend a hand to those who have stumbled. Without your indwelling of us, we would be little more than hollow shells. You, Lord, define and infuse our journey with purpose.

The last page of the chapter is about to turn. Another day is done. As we reflect on how the day has unfolded, what we've discovered that may be of value for tomorrow, and what amends need to be made, we look to you for the gift of discernment. We look to you for wisdom. Light fades to night and mystery shrouds what's left of this day like a warm blanket. Faith in your faithfulness has allowed us to make peace with mystery. We fear not what may come in the night or what tomorrow holds. The only certainty we rely on is your abiding presence, and in this we experience peace.

Morning, noon, and night we praise your holy name! Amen.

PRAYERS OF GRATITUDE

"Rejoice always, pray without ceasing,
give thanks in all circumstances,
for this is the will of God in Christ Jesus for you."

I THESSALONIANS 5:16-18

Give Thanks in All Circumstances

There are times when words alone are not enough. When I'm so grateful that anything I say falls short before I complete the sentence. This is when my prayer of gratitude turns to a song of praise as I boldly sing the "Doxology." There are no truer words than, "Praise God from whom all blessings flow..." Once I've sung the "Amen." Words of gratitude freely flow. It's as if gratitude requires a prelude of praise on which words alone can waft their way to God.

We are instructed in scripture to give thanks in all circumstances. This doesn't mean that we must give thanks *for* the circumstance, but we are to give thanks during or while in the circumstance. I learned the divine wisdom of this instruction one afternoon in the pediatrician's office several years ago when Greg was in high school.

Greg had a leg injury that started off as a deep bruise. There was a school trip that he had been looking forward to, so we got him a set of crutches and waved goodbye as he boarded the bus. Several days later when he returned, the bruise had spread over most of his calf. It was evident that he needed to be seen by a doctor. We thought it must be broke. We never imagined that it could be worse until the doctor said, "I hope we can save the leg."

I don't know what it feels like to go into shock, but I'm sure I was on the verge of it. Greg was on the exam table. The doctor had stepped out of the room to call an orthopedic surgeon and I had called Gene to say, "Come quick." I then moved to be next to Greg, who was visibly shaking. I had no idea what to do, until I heard myself say, "All I know to do is pray." He agreed and I began to pray. This was when I experienced the Spirit stepping up to pray when no words were forthcoming. The first words I head come from my mouth were, "Thank you..." "Thank you, God, that we are here in this doctor's office," followed by, "Thank you that the doctor knows us and cares about Greg and will do what is best," and again, "Thank you for the surgeon he is calling..." On and on I prayed, one thank you after another. I lost count, but I know when I was prompted to say, "Amen," there was a degree of peace that had settled over us. Nothing had changed—no plan of action or next step had been announced. Greg and I were still the only two in the room—nothing had changed and yet *we* had been changed. We were still very concerned but calm. The sense of shock had dissipated.

Gene arrived in time for the doctor to fill him in on the situation and tell us how to get to the surgeon's office. Thankfully, the orthopedic doctor was able to offer assurance that his leg was not in jeopardy at that time. There were non-surgical procedures that could be followed and, hopefully, he would be out of danger soon. Thankfully, the procedures worked, and Greg was back on his feet in a few days. All that remained was a large bruise on his leg that didn't disappear for the next few years— yes, years—but at least he had his leg—thank the Lord!

God had transformed our panic to peace through the gift of gratitude. Just saying and hearing the words, "Thank you, thank you , thank you..." over and over proved to be calming. Since that day, I have trusted in the power of gratitude to evoke peace in desperate moments, or when people are frightened. Often, when praying with someone while they are in pre-op awaiting surgery, my pray begins with "Thank you," and ends the same. There are prayers for various occasions, but a prayer of gratitude is always appropriate—in all circumstances.

Oh yes, and on the way home, I sang the Doxology with tears streaming down my face!   *"Rejoice always, pray without ceasing, give thanks in all circumstances, for this is the will of God in Christ Jesus for you."* I Thessalonians 5:16-18

Gratitude Begins with "Thank You"

We may consider the expression, "Fake it 'til you make it," poor advice until we realize that this is what we advocate every time we prompt children to say "thank you" or encourage them to blow a kiss, bow their heads when they pray, and many other desirable behaviors.

In other words, gratitude is not genetic. Some people are not "naturally" more grateful than others. Gratitude is a manner of being—a mindset that has been nurtured from birth. Gracious people probably grew up around grateful people. By modeling the behavior of those whose approval they most sought, they became grateful. Gratitude is initially a learned behavior, that we trust will one day become a motivating source—a true reflection of the soul.

When Greg and Julia were very young, we began teaching them how to behave as grateful children. Someone would do something kind for them or give them a gift and we would say, "Say thank you." They would then parrot back, "Thank you." and we would reinforce their response with kind words, a thumbs-up, or wink of the eye. For several months, each time they received a compliment or act of kindness, we would remind them to say thank you.

Eventually, we shifted from telling them what to say, to posing the question, "What do you say?" to which they would respond, "Thank you." They had learned the desired response. Finally, the day came when, without provocation, we heard them say thank you on their own! What a joy it was to hear them say these thoughtful words without having to be told. I remember being so delighted that I immediately said, "Thank you for saying thank you!" and I meant it. I was sincerely grateful that they were behaving as grateful children—whether they were *feeling* grateful or simply offering the desired response. Either way, I knew that the day would come when their feelings would catch up with their behavior. They would live into their identity as children of God.

C.S. Lewis wrote an essay for a radio broadcast that then became chapter seven in his book, *Mere Christianity*. The essay is entitled *"Let's Pretend."* In it he clarifies the difference between pretense that is deceitful, and pretense that leads to a positive reality. He claims that the only way we actually become grateful, friendly, generous, or kind, is by behaving as if we already are what we want to become.

When we think about it, this is what we advocate as Christians. We look to Jesus as our model for how to treat others, and then we attempt to live in the same manner—whether we feel loving toward our enemies or not. Eventually, as we continue to "do what Jesus would do," we become Christ-like. This is the transforming power of God at work within us, taking what we offer—our actions—and transforming our emotions, feelings, and desires to match.

The Apostle Paul expressed it like this, when he wrote to the Galatians, "...*it is no longer I who live, but it is Christ who lives in me...*" Gal. 2:20. Seeking to be grateful is a worthy pursuit and, by the grace of God, it's attainable. It begins with how we respond and treat each other. Another action that leads to sincere gratitude is counting our blessings—or making a list of things and people, experiences for which we are grateful. This one simple action has been proven to be a healthy exercise for our brain as well as our soul.

A favorite passage worthy of learning by heart is Colossians 3:12-17. It begins, *"As God's chosen ones, holy and beloved..."* The passage then instructs us to "clothe" ourselves with compassion, kindness, humility, and many other behaviors that are fitting of God's chosen. It ends with this final instruction *"And whatever you do, in word or deed, do everything in the name of the Lord Jesus, giving thanks to God the Father through him."*

PRAYER

You take the words we learn by rote and infuse them with feeling, Lord, and we become your grateful people. Filled with gratitude we seek ways to express it, and you provide us opportunities to serve in your name, sing your praises, and bear witness to your goodness.

Thank you, God, for the gift of gratitude and the joy it brings us as we offer you our thanks and praise. Amen.

Presbyterian and Proud of It

The Presbyterian Church (USA) has experienced a mass exodus over the past several years, as have other denominations. Nonetheless, this has forced many of us to examine our understanding of who we are and what we believe—myself included.

One of the many reasons I choose to live out my faith in Christ through the Presbyterian Church (USA) is because I appreciate that we are a connectional church. We have a rich heritage of linking arms with each other and with other denominations that huddle right alongside us under the umbrella of Christianity. Together we serve God by helping those in need around the world. That's just one of the reasons I continue to be a member of the Presbyterian Church (USA), but the reason I *am* a Presbyterian is much more intrinsic.

I am a Presbyterian because it's here that my parents had me baptized when I was six months old. It is here in this branch of Christ's church that I was first welcomed into the household of God and nurtured in the faith.

It is here, in the Presbyterian Church, that I heard the story of baby Jesus's birth for the first time, and eventually learned to sing "Silent Night"—even the hardest line of all: "…round yon virgin, Mother and Child."

It is here, in the Presbyterian Church, that I learned that God made the world and also made me, and that Trinity isn't just the name of an oak tree at Buffalo Gap Encampment, but stands for Father, Son and Holy Spirit.

It is here that I learned to sing "Jesus Loves Me" and also "I'm a Little Tea Pot" (I'm still not sure why Ta-Tee thought we needed to learn that one, but it remains a favorite, nonetheless), and it is here that I developed a love for hymns—to the extent that my piano teacher allowed me to play one each year for the recital.

It is here, in the Presbyterian Church, that I learned by heart the 23rd Psalm, The Lord's Prayer, the Beatitudes, and funny words like debts and debtors, narthex, undercroft, doxology, and catechism. It is here, in the Presbyterian Church, that I took communion for the first time, read scripture from the pulpit as a teenager and for the first time knew I wanted to do it again and again. It is here that I learned the power of prayer, and the ministry of presence, and here that I have heard God's call time and again.

It is here where I have experienced church as family, and here, in the Presbyterian Church, where I know what it is to be rooted in the faith, bound by the love of God, saved by the grace extended through Jesus Christ, and sensed the Holy Spirit's abiding presence. It is here, in the Presbyterian Church (USA), that I experience home.

PRAYER

Heavenly Father—Abba, what a blessing it is to be your children—to be rooted in your love and growing in your grace. What a blessing it is to know that though the winds of change may rattle our windows and overturn a few of our dreams, your love for us is rock solid, and your faithfulness cannot be shaken. For this we give thanks. Amen.

A Full-Circle Moment

The room was quiet but for the gurgling sound coming from the oxygen device over the hospital bed. The curtains were drawn and the room dimly lit. I entered slowly. There she lay—a frail figure wadded up in the center of the bed. "Juanita?" I whispered. "Juanita?"

Suddenly her big blue eyes opened wide, and quickly I identified myself, "It's Janice." And before I could say more, she began chattering incessantly, with no evident of slowing to draw a breath. What was I to do? I had awakened her from peaceful sleep and now she was wound up and I was powerless to calm her. I couldn't just walk away, but to begin a prayer while she was still speaking seemed inappropriate. Then an idea came to mind. This precious little lady had been the cradle roll teacher for years—my cradle roll teacher. No doubt she had held me in her arms many a Sunday morning and rocked me back and forth. Perhaps she had sung to me. What if I were to try singing to her? Softly, I began to hum "Jesus Loves Me." I hummed all the way through it one time then began singing it slowly. Was it my imagination or was she quieting? I repeated the song one more time. By the third time through the song, little Miss Juanita was sound asleep again. All that could be heard was the gurgling of the oxygen device in the dimly lit room.

"Thank you, God." There by her bedside I was overcome with gratitude. I was so grateful for the gift of belonging to the family of faith my entire life; grateful for this full-circle moment when I was given the opportunity to calm this sweet little woman, and sing her to sleep, just as she had done for me many times.

PRAYER

As members of the Body of Christ we are one with you, Lord, and one with each other, Thank you for creating us for community, for it is through our life together that we come to recognize you as you move among us. Working through us, equipping, inspiring, and comforting your children, you draw us closer and closer to you, and in turn, to one another.

By the power of your Holy Spirit, Lord, bind us together as family. May we never take this beautiful gift of community for granted or attempt to go it alone. Here, in the midst of your people, may we discover the font of every blessing, the well-spring of joy, and the fullness of life. Here, in the midst of your people, may we experience your presence as we serve side by side, sing praises to your name, and offer a sympathizing tear. Here, in the midst of your people, may your joy be made complete in us. Amen.

The Shadow of Death

One day while in the chapel of the Alzheimer's unit where our mother lived for four years, my brother Ron noticed Psalm 23 framed and hanging on the wall. Having memorized it as a child, he knew the words by heart, but on this day one phrase struck a new chord. "Yea, though I walk through the valley of the shadow of death…" It occurred to him that "the shadow of death" was a good description for Alzheimer's and this is where Mom was— in the valley of the shadow of death. Not death, but the shadow of death, was veiling her mind a little more each day. Four years after her death in 2007, I wrote a reflection inspired by Ron's revelation.

"Walking Through the Valley of the Shadows of Her Mind"

Looming fears and grief disguised she hopes none will notice as she quietly disappears behind her tear-filled eyes. Her tight-lipped smile holds at bay stammering words she longs to say. Tangled vines and brittle leaves are like memories being crushed under foot—her memories that continue to crumble one day at a time. Her vision dims though the light still shines, making it difficult to find her way as she passes through the valley of the shadows of her mind.

Facing west, the sun hangs low. Long shadows veil the now parched past. Over the hill and down below lays the barren desert and her dreaded foe. It's a desolate place and one of woe, nonetheless it's where she's destined to go.

Minutes tick away. Days drone by. Weeks meld into months that are stacking up one after another. Silently we wonder, how many years will she have to suffer?

Stumbling more, her steps slow to a shuffle. Loved ones line the lonely path, straining to help in any way possible. Efforts are futile to halt the inevitable. This progressive, irreversible, degenerative disease will conquer her body but not her soul.

The sun tops the horizon as these words prove true: *"Weeping may linger for the night, but joy comes with the morning!"* Psalm 30:5 Her arduous trek is now complete. Crossing the divine threshold, she's entered a pristine land where there are no more tangled vines or brittle leaves. Memories no longer crumble or fade from sight. In this land, the Light has overcome night, and shadows of the mind are no more.

PRAYER

Gracious and Loving Lord,

We fall into your strong arms that have held us up over these last few years. The awareness of your presence has been our peace, and the faith you've given us has been our shield against fear. As Mother's memory was being chipped away a little at a time, we knew there would come a day when she would not recognize us, and our voices would be foreign to her. I was convinced that nothing could be as horrible as being forgotten by my own mother. Yet, when the day came, you were there, and I realized you had been preparing me all along when she politely asked, "How's Janice?" and without hesitating, I smiled and replied, "I'm Janice and I'm fine." It was true, Lord, I was fine, thanks to you.

When words would no longer come, you gave me ears to hear "I love you," through the expression in her eyes, and the way she gently patted my hand just as she had always done. Thank you for answering my prayer for her to feel safe so that she could be content. Thank you for the reminder that with this thief in the night, we have only one moment to treasure at a time.

As Mom made the journey through the valley of shadows, grief was never far behind. Those of us who walked alongside her had our run-ins with grief, but we were never overtaken because you were always with us each step of the way.

You, Lord, have turned our night to day. Though we grieve, it is not as those who have no hope. Our faith and our hope are in Christ and the promise of everlasting life. By your mercy, Mom's suffering has ended and she is now at home with you and all the saints forevermore, and for this we are grateful. Amen.

Making Peace with the Mystery of God

Some people are certain that to have control is to be in power and to be in power is to be secure. However, as I see it, the notion of possessing power and control is nothing more than a mirage in the desert.

Thirsty and weary, we see water in the distance—an oasis perhaps! If we can only get there, we will find shade from the scorching sun, and refreshment from cool, clear water. Digging deep within our reservoir of energy and willpower, we run toward it, but it seems no matter how far we travel, the mirage remains beyond us. If we ever think we're gaining on it, the edges of the pool recess and suddenly it vanishes. We then realize it was never really there.

Maybe having experienced a few mirages in my life— both real and metaphorically—has helped me make peace with the mystery of God. As long as I trust in the goodness and sovereignty of God, I don't need all the details of what's around the corner or over the hill. As long as I rely on the Spirit's abiding presence and willingness to guide and correct me, I can continue to move into the future with some degree of confidence. Sure, wrongdoing and natural disasters will create obstacles, but as long as I believe in the power of God to help me overcome, outsmart, or endure them, all will be well with my soul. Also essential to the acceptance of mystery is knowing that God is beyond humanity's ability to fully comprehend. This assures me that God is not vulnerable and, therefore, cannot be manipulated.

So here are the four key assurances that have allowed me to be at peace with the mystery of God and to hopefully be a non-anxious presence in my corner of the world:

- The big picture and end of the story belong to God.
- God is loving, kind, forgiving, and all things good.
- God has the power to do whatever God wants.
- God cannot be controlled or manipulated.

With these convictions, I not only tolerate but have made peace with the mystery of God.

PRAYER

Almighty God,

We know you only in part—only to the extent that you reveal yourself to us—yet we know enough to turn to you in prayer. Ironically, the more we learn of you, the more we realize how little we know. Yet with this revelation comes a peace—the peace of knowing that your greatness exceeds our comprehension. Because we know of your plan to reconcile all creation to you, and because we know of your goodness, love, and power, we can be at peace with the mystery.

Thank you for the gift of faith that enables us to believe. Thank you for opening our hearts to receive Christ, and thank you for blessing us with an ongoing awareness your abiding presence now and always. Amen.

Predestination and God's GPS

Christians can spend an inordinate amount of mental energy and angst trying to define predestination. For those who trust the Bible to be the authoritative word of God, predestination cannot be denied. (Read Romans 8). However, a person's understanding of this doctrine has been debated for generations, and probably will be until God's kingdom is restored on this earth!

Below are a few of my personal thoughts on the topic. I'm quick to add that I am not so arrogant as to claim them to be the final word on the subject.

By presenting them, I am simply offering "food for thought" and hopefully it will whet your appetite for thinking through this doctrine for yourself—if you are so inclined:

- If anyone is concerned about predestination, this is evidence that they are among the elect. However, the converse of this statement does *not* hold true. To make this assumption is bizarre logic. Not all people are curious about the topic, nor do they care to spend time debating it. This in no way indicates they are cast out of God's household.

- No one is chosen for damnation. In fact, it is God's

desire that every knee shall bend and acknowledge Christ as Lord (Philippians 2:9-11). It is God's plan that all creation shall be reconciled to God through Jesus Christ (2 Corinthians 5:11-21). All are welcome!

- God's plan for salvation through Christ has been foreordained. We have the assurance that in Christ we are saved. Maybe God has other means of drawing all people to God's self, but what we know as Christians is that Christ is the way. If God so chooses for others to join us, it's God's prerogative to grant salvation to whomever God desires. Far be it from me to argue with God about such matters.

- As a Christian, who understands that we are called to love everyone—including our enemies — the purist expression of this love is to hope and pray that God *will* make a way for all to join us at the Messianic Feast!

- Because God has chosen for humanity to have the freedom to make decisions, it's possible that some may stubbornly refuse God's invitation. I believe this will sadden God and therefore sadden all of us who pray for God's will to be done on earth as it is in heaven.

God's GPS

It's God's will that we one day join the Church Triumphant. This is our ultimate destination, and there are a number of routes we can take. Granted, some are more direct, with fewer obstacles, but we are free to choose the path we follow. Whichever route we choose, there will still be many intersections and decisions to be made along the way.

Because we are human, we will make a wrong turn now and then. Thankfully, the GPS never loses sight of us. Within moments, it recalculates the course to get us back on track—no shaming and no lecture. It simply recalculates the route based on where we are. Some of us will makes choices that lead us through the desert, or over rocky mountain passes. Some of us may end up driving in circles. However, one way or another, God will lead us home. There we will take our place in the heavenly realm with all the saints who have gone before us! What a day of rejoicing this will be!

PRAYER

Gracious and loving God, thank you for the gift of faith that makes it possible for us to believe what we have not seen, and trust in your goodness and love for all creation.

Thank you that our salvation rests not in our hands, but in yours. It is you who has provided the way and it is you who will lead us home.

Out of gratitude for your ultimate plan for renewing the face of the earth, and reconciling all creation to you through Christ, may we joyfully share the good news with all you lead our way. Amen.

Do What You Have the Power to Do

"What does the Lord require of you? To act justly, and to love mercy and to walk humbly with your God." (Micah 6:8) I have quoted this verse, sung it as a round in worship, and romanticized it in poetry, but when called to live it, I find it to be time consuming, complicated, and confounding.

I was reminded of this one Monday morning several years ago when one of our childcare workers showed up with Maggie. The childcare worker had insisted that Maggie and her two young children come with her to work that morning, saying, "I'll take you to my church. They'll know what to do. They'll help you." Just hearing what she had told this young woman made me a little uneasy. Would we know what to do? Would we be able to help her?

Maggie had problems—big problems. She had no home, no job, no car, and less than two dollars in her pocket. What she did have in her favor was a good friend who knew from experience that when you're in trouble, go to the church. So, here stood Maggie and her two young children and I had less than ten minutes before the women would be arriving for the final lesson based on a book by Helen Bruch Pearson, entitled, *Do What You Have the Power to Do: A Study of Six New Testament Women.*

Although the study did not center on the oppression of women in Biblical times, we had been reminded week after week that women had it tough back in Jesus' day. We were reminded that Jesus broke the norms on several occasions and, by so doing, elevated the status of women—at least in the eyes of some. We acknowledged the courage of the women who made themselves vulnerable by taking risks, being in places where they weren't allowed, speaking to those to whom they were forbidden to speak, and reaching out in faith to Jesus—the one who had the power to heal. What had we learned? As God would have it, today would be the test. The first lesson we would learn is that some things have not changed.

Maggie was shaking, tearful, and scared. No way could I turn my back on her and her children. What could I do in the next few minutes that would give her a ray of hope? I could hire her to help with the children—her children—for the next couple of hours until the Bible study was over. Now she had a job, and it was time to begin the lesson on *Do What You Have the Power to Do.*

After enjoying coffee and pecan caramel Danish, followed by a prayer, I began the lesson. Not far into it Maggie's young son began to wail, and it was only getting louder. The women were curious. What was going on across the hall? Why the hysteria? Suddenly, as uncontrolled as the young boy's cry, the lesson of the day tumbled from my heart: "Here we sit in the security of our lives, with the luxury of gathering each Monday morning to study and enjoy fellowship, while across the hall is a woman and her two children who live each day on the edge." I then whispered some of the details of Maggie's dire situation, and also told of the childcare worker's confidence that we would know what to do. I then said, "Now ladies, it's our turn to do what *we* have the power to do."

Immediately, the women began reaching for their purses—not to leave—but to do what they had the power to do. Twenties, tens, and fives were tossed on the table. The money would certainly help, but money wasn't enough and this group knew it. They started brainstorming about housing, job openings, childcare. This was just the beginning. For the next five months, our church family embraced Maggie and her children. Not only were daily needs being met, but so, too, were part-time employment, medical care, transportation and, of course, Christmas gifts.

Maggie had found refuge in the church and, because members of the church did what they had the power to do, Maggie's hope had been restored.

There's more to the story, and because this isn't a fairy tale, not everything turned out "happily ever after." Maggie and her children were ultimately relocated to an undisclosed location to avoid future abuse. The night she left, I was able to give her a letter, with the instruction, "When you get where you're going, find a Presbyterian Church and give them this letter." Like Paul, I had written a letter of introduction, trusting that when the pastor read it, they would help Maggie and the children get on their feet.

A few months passed, then one day the phone rang. It was from a Presbyterian church in another state. The person on the line asked me to hold. The next voice I heard was Maggie's! She began by saying, "We did what you said. We found this church, and just like all of you, they are helping us." They, too, were putting into action the teachings of Christ—they, too, were doing what they had the power to do. Praise the Lord!

PRAYER

In the midst of chaos you call the church to rise up and do what it has the power to do. Thank you for the compassion, faith, and courage, you've given the church that compels your followers to take risks and make sacrifices for the sake of those who are suffering. Amen.

A Man of God

My father was a man of integrity, reserve, kind and loyal. At his funeral, he was compared to Joseph, the earthly father of Jesus. We know little about Joseph from scripture, but I've always imagined him to be a quiet man, who lived his faith with little fanfare. The same could be said about my earthly father.

What we do know is that Joseph was a Jewish carpenter who faithfully honored Torah, the Jewish traditions, and holy feasts. Joseph is described as a righteous man—a man of faith—who heeded God's instruction as conveyed to him in dreams and through the voice of angels. Joseph was a man of God. So, too, was my dad.

My earliest memory of a theological discussion with my dad was when I was four years old. It took place on a Sunday afternoon with Dad seated in his chair—the green chair, as we called it. Dad was "resting his eyes," as he used to say, while I stood by waiting as long as I could, before shaking his arm. I was so eager to tell him what I had learned in Sunday school that morning. Our teacher had taught us a song about our Father, and I knew he would love it!

As soon as I touched him he opened his eyes, and that was all the invitation I needed to climb up in his lap.

Promptly I announced that I had learned a new song and it was about him! Then I began singing it. I don't remember the title, but it was something about My Father, strong and kind. When I finished, my dad smiled, as he always did, and thanked me for singing it for him. He then, to my surprise, told me that the song wasn't about him. Oh yes it was, I argued! The words described him perfectly.

That's when my dad drew me close, and thoughtfully explained that we have another father—a heavenly Father, who is always with us, and loves us no matter what.

Sadly, there are too many earthly fathers whose behavior and manner have tainted the title. For this reason, some children and adults resist thinking of God as "Father." Therefore, I make a point of referring to God as "*heavenly* Father," and I stress that unlike our earthly fathers, our heavenly Father is the *perfect* Father—the Father who always loves us, forgives us, and calls us by name. Our heavenly Father is patient and wants the best for us—always. Our heavenly Father hears us anytime we cry and welcomes us anytime we want to talk. Our heavenly Father will never hurt us, abandon us, or turn us away. Our heavenly Father is the one who assures us that nothing in all creation can ever separate us from his love—the love we experience through Christ our Lord.

Believing all these attributes about our heavenly Father has been easy for me, thanks to my earthly father, who modeled what it is to live a life entrusted to God. My earthly father's deep, abiding faith in God's faithfulness resulted in a countenance of peace and contentment in all circumstances. Like our heavenly Father, my earthly father's love knew no bounds. Without question, he was as a man of God.

PRAYER

Heavenly Father, you have blessed our family with an earthly father, whose faithfulness in all things has given us the courage to trust that you are good.

His strong gentle way has given us the confidence to express compassion.

His perseverance in all situations has given us the strength to carry on.

His loyalty to family and friends has given us respect for others.

His deep abiding faith in your love for us has freed us to live with joy.

In his life and in his death, our father has given us a model for living.

For this we give thanks. Amen.

The Brownie Story

It was one of those days. As much as I enjoyed including Julia and Greg in whatever activities I had to do, today was one of those days when I was eager to check tasks off the list.

It wouldn't take more than seven minutes to mix up a batch of brownies—as long as I was on my own without extra little helping hands. So, quietly I took the bowl from the cabinet, gathered the ingredients, and no sooner had I cracked the first egg, I could hear Julia running down the hall.

Julia loved to make brownies—probably because I let her "lick the bowl"—but also because she was four and what four-year-old doesn't enjoy helping? Entering the kitchen, she went straight to the kitchen table and began dragging a chair across the room to the counter where I was working. Climbing up onto the chair, she was ready to take charge.

She had been able to crack an egg without getting shell in the batter since she was three so, short of reading the recipe, there wasn't much she couldn't do. Reluctantly I relinquished the wooden spoon and held the bowl as she began to vigorously stir. It wasn't long before some batter sloshed over the side of the bowl and I started to reclaim the spoon, when I had an epiphany.

In that split second, as I saw the joy Julia took in helping me, I realized how akin this might be to how it feels when God invites and allows us to join in the work that God is doing. We know that in the blink of an eye, God could bring to fruition his plan, but instead, God patiently allows us to help.

It was in that moment that I realized the joy of service and the gratitude for being allowed to be engaged in God's work. It was in that moment that I realized how loving it is to let others work beside us—especially our little ones.

PRAYER

"O what love you lavish on us that we should be called your children, and that is who we are." 1 John 3:1.

Heavenly Father, we thank you for generous hearts in little bodies that want nothing more than to be given the chance to serve. Thank you for little hands eager to learn, and big eyes filled with wonder and awe.

In their wrinkled brows we see how earnestly they attempt new feats, like cracking an egg, or learning to use a hammer. We remember the genuine desire we had at their age to please a parent or grandparent, a caregiver, or older siblings.

Thank you for young ones who teach us life lessons, like the importance of play. Grant us the patience to put our own endeavors on hold, and the energy to accept their invitation to join them in the magical world of their imaginations.

As we tell them the stories of Jesus, we pray that they will embrace him as their own, and throughout their lifetime make it their aim to follow in his footsteps. You, Lord, are the giver of all good gifts. Out of your storehouse of faith, you share with your little ones. Please give them, and each of us, a full measure to last a lifetime. Like yeast, may the faith you give us be a living faith that grows over time. May we incorporate it into daily living and cling to it in crisis.

Heavenly Father, thank you for welcoming us into your household—for claiming us as your children— through Jesus Christ, in whose name we pray. Amen.

PRAYERS OF INTERCESSION

*"…Love your enemies and pray for those who
persecute you, so that you may be children of your Father in
heaven; for he makes his sun rise on the
evil and on the good, and sends rain on the righteous and on
the unrighteous…And if you greet only
your brothers and sisters, what more are you
doing than others?"*

MATTHEW 5:44-45, 47

Prayers for the People

So often in life, when family or friends are hurt, we can't fix what's broken—especially when it comes to matters of the heart, or physical ailments that require more than a bandage. It's a helpless feeling when there's nothing to offer but to say, "I'll pray for you." Be assured, there are times when praying on behalf of others is the absolute best we have to give.

In a casual conversation with a friend one day, she wondered aloud if people really do pray when they say they will. Her question prompted me to wonder how many others have wondered the same. It also gave me an idea. Rather than just saying I would pray, I began the practice of praying on the spot in the form of an email or text message. Many times, I have pulled into a parking lot and prayed in this manner—sending it to the one who made the request as an assurance that people—at least many of us—really do pray for them and their loved ones when we say we will.

Interceding on behalf of others is a privilege and greatly appreciated by those who may be unable to pray for themselves or loved ones for one reason or another. There are times when people feel that prayer is futile. As far as they can see, God has ignored their prayers and they have no desire to pray. Consumed with grief, numb from shock, or while the crisis is raging, are a few other times. Two examples come to mind.

The first was many years ago when a friend's adult son was in ICU. I raced to the hospital as soon as I learned the news and asked the question most of us ask, "Is there anything I can do?" Usually the answer is "no," but my friend surprised me. She said, "Yes," explaining that she felt it was important for someone to be at his bedside, praying over him at all times, but as much as she wanted to be the one, she was concerned that she wasn't emotionally strong enough to do so at the time. She then asked, "Will you go in for me and pray for him?" I was so touched by her request. So, for the next few hours, I stood by this young man's side and prayed as his mother requested. To this day, anytime I have visited a patient in ICU, I think of my friend and the trust she placed in me to pray over her son at a time when she didn't feel that she could.

Another time, a woman came to see me. I could tell she was exhausted. She then shared the serious concern she had for her family and that she was obsessively praying for them—over and over the same prayer all day. I wanted to help and I knew she needed rest. An idea sprang to mind. I stood in front of her, put my hands out, and asked, "Will you let me carry your burden for the rest of today so you can get some rest?" I then promised that if she would let me, I would take over praying for her family all day. She practically fell into my arms with relief, and thankfully entrusted her concerns to me for the rest of the day, promising that she would let me do the praying and she would rest. What a privilege it was to intercede in prayer for her that day. Over the years, I heard her tell this story, so I knew it meant as much to her as it did to me.

I hope these examples will be of benefit, and I pray—I really do—that you will be blessed as you give of your time and heart to pray for others—particularly those who cannot pray for themselves or those they love.

BLESSING

Blessed are you, who pray for others—for family and friends—when their minds are on overload and their feelings numbed by the severity of the situation.

Blessed are you who know that a silent prayer is just as powerful as one proclaimed aloud, and that when all we have to offer are sighs and moans, the Spirit intercedes and prays for us.

Blessed are you, who reverently and faithfully carry the burden of your neighbor when her knees are sore and her voice hoarse from praying through the night.

Blessed are you, my friends, who honor your promise to pray. Amen.

People of Faith Carry On

"God is our refuge and strength. A very present help in trouble. Therefore, we will not fear, though the earth should change... The nations are in an uproar, the kingdoms totter; God utters his voice, the earth melts. The Lord of hosts is with us; the God of Jacob is our refuge." Psalm 46:1, 5-7

The second Tuesday morning of September each year was once reserved for the Presbyterian Women's annual prayer retreat. Reverend Nan Swanson, pastor of First Presbyterian Church in Snyder, Texas, was driving over to lead the retreat. Nan was planning to introduce our group to Taizé prayer that originated in Taizé, France. This distinctive, contemplative prayer is characterized by simple refrains that are sung reverently and repetitively. The desired result is that in addition to communicating with God, the prayer will reside in the worshipers' hearts and can be called to mind and sung at any time. Over the years, I have found this to be true.

While the prayer is reminiscent of ancient Gregorian chants, it came about during WWII, for the primary purpose of praying for world peace. How ironic it was that this was to be the program for the prayer retreat on this particular Tuesday—a day that would live in infamy in the minds of U.S. citizens and people around the world. The date was September 11, 2001.

Even those who were in elementary school at the time can probably say what they were doing when they heard the news. If there was a television within sight, people watched in horror as the attack on the World Trade Center unfolded.

When I first heard that a commercial plane had struck the World Trade Center, I thought it was an accident. When the second tower was struck, it was obvious that our country was under attack. I remember thinking, "This isn't possible! Wars are fought on foreign soil—not here!"

My initial reaction was to cancel the prayer retreat, but before I could draw the next breath, I realized that coming together at the church to pray was exactly what we needed to do.

As the women began arriving, the typical chatter and laughter was muted. The room was practically silent. Nan began the program. The opening refrain she had chosen weeks earlier could not have been more relevant. Its message was one of calm affirmation: Nothing can trouble nor frighten those who seek God. The words and the tune were as soothing as a fragrant balm. Over and over, we sang the simple refrain until it saturated our souls, calming our spirit and transforming our panic into peace.

That morning, trusting in God's presence and

guidance, and leaning heavily on our faith in God's faithfulness, goodness, and sovereignty, we chose to carry on, because that's what people of faith do. We carry on.

PRAYER

We recognize, Lord, that when prejudiced minds taunt, and dare, those in search of significance, they become easy prey. Like marionettes in the puppet master's hands, they can be made to dance to any tune. So, even though we hate what they have done, we pray for the pilots, with strings attached, who carried out the evil instructions of those who planned the atrocious acts of destruction.

We pray for the little children, loving spouses, siblings, and parents who mourn their deaths, just as we pray for the families of men, women, and children who innocently, and violently, died at the hands of these same enemies for whom we pray.

Only you, O Sovereign God, have the power to sort through the rubble and ashes, to raise up a phoenix of redemption for your devasted world.

With heavy hearts, we pray for strength, discernment, courage, and a desire for peace that will be necessary to have a willingness to forgive. With faith, we wait and watch for brighter days. Amen.

Prayer for Soldiers

Dozens and dozens of homemade cookies, baked by members of the church family, were mailed to deployed military personnel following 9/11. All were either members or had family who were members of our congregation. The following is the letter and prayer that was to be included with each box of cookies.

Letter...

As we were placing the mounds of cookie dough onto the baking sheet, we thought of how they reminded us of you and those with whom you are serving: The dough is a combination of various ingredients. Each is needed for a specific role, such as eggs for leavening, flour for structure, extracts for flavor. Any one of the ingredients by itself is not a cookie. It takes all of them working together—just like you.

Also like you, these cookies have been prepared, placed in formation on the baking sheet, and sent into the heat. Now they are ready to serve—as are you.

May God continue to watch over and bless you as you strive to carry out your mission.

PRAYER

You hold the whole world in your hands, Lord, and right now it seems very fragile. We give thanks for the men and women who have stepped forward to try and mend what's broken. Please protect them as they serve, and may their efforts be honored both where they are and by the American people they represent.

With each bite of cookie, remind them that there are mothers, fathers, brothers, sisters, aunts and uncles, grandparents and spouses, children, best friends and co-workers, and members of their church family who are praying for them and eagerly await their return. Amen.

A Prayer for Our Nation

In September of 2015 I was invited to offer the prayer at a fundraiser for Global Samaritan, whose stated mission is "...to demonstrate God's love by providing logistics and need-based solutions through partners helping people who are facing hardship, crisis, or disaster." The keynote speaker for the event was former President George W. Bush. The following is the prayer offered that evening.

PRAYER

"Our God, our help in ages past, our hope for years to come..."

With confidence in your goodness, faith in your faithfulness, and humble gratitude for entrusting to Global Samaritan the important work that goes on behind the scenes—the necessary labor of preparing the way and equipping others to serve as Christ's ambassadors—we give thanks.

Here in this land of the free and the brave, prompt us to set our sights well beyond our own backyards and borders. Expand our horizons and dispel any prejudices that threaten our generosity and reverence for all life. May we become known around the world as a land of compassion and reconciliation.

Grant us the courage to attempt the unlikely, humility to serve without recognition, and a full measure of infectious joy, so that all with whom we share this journey will join in a song of praise for all your help in ages past and hope for years to come. Amen.

Memorial Day

God works wonders through the prayers of God's people. On Memorial Day we give thanks for the freedoms we enjoy in this country and for all who have contributed to the preservation of them.

Out of gratitude for the blessings we enjoy, may we be intentional about doing what we can to meet the needs of those who have less opportunities to achieve their dreams.

PRAYER

On this Memorial Day weekend, Lord, we are mindful of the thousands of young men and women over the years who have risked their lives that we might have the freedoms we so easily take for granted.

We pray for the families of those who never returned from war—whose lives were cut short—whose dreams died with them on the battlefield. And we certainly pray for those who survived war but continue to be haunted by what they saw and experienced. Be their peace, Lord, and heal the wounds that none can see.

We look forward to the day when enmity between nations will be no more; when the spirit of cooperation, and compassion, will be valued, and sought. We trust that one day peace on earth will prevail. What a day of rejoicing it will be!

Give us the courage to listen for your lead and the willingness to follow—whether it be across the room to make peace within our own household, or the other side of the world to demonstrate your love in action.

In the meantime, kindle within us a fire that warms the heart and softens our insistence that we know best in all circumstances. May we have the humility, and compassion, to help people get what they need, like clean water, medical care, food, and justice.

Grow your church, Lord, and by the power of your Holy Spirit, may the church be a people of joy, freedom, convictions, kindness, hospitality, empathy, and compassion. May the world know that we are Christians by the love we have for one another and, also, for those who oppose us.

We pray this in the name of the One who continues to welcome sinners to his table—the One who welcomes us. Amen.

A Prayer for the New Year

The first day of a new year is one of my favorite days of the year. It's like a blanket of fresh snow as far as the eye can see. Pristine an unblemished, the new year represents an opportunity to start over. Nothing has been wasted and there are no regrets. It's a fresh beginning and all is possible!

The first day of the new year invites the imagination to come out and play! Dream big! Make bold plans and ambitious resolutions if that's what pleases you. The only goal for today is to imagine what could be.

Another practice that gets the year off to a grand start is to make a gratitude list—a long list. Invites all you're spending the day with to add to the list. There's research to support that gratitude actually can boost the neurotransmitter serotonin and activate the positive, making expressing gratitude a healthy practice.

PRAYER

As we near the threshold of another year, Lord, we pause to look over our shoulder.

Oh, the surprises we eagerly recall! Marked by your divine fingerprints, it's evident you handled all. And —as we have learned to expect—the year in review had its share of heartaches and tears, frustrations, and fears. Yet to be certain, there were plenty of bright spots and memory-making moments. For this we give thanks.

Looking ahead to the new year, we do so aware that only you know what the future holds. Only you know the full measure of grief we'll bear. Only you know the wonderful treasures yet untold. So, we look to you, Lord, to guide us on our way. Remind us of your presence each and every day. Nudge us when we get complacent. Cajole and enthuse us to do your will. And with a song on our lips, and a prayer in our hearts, bless us now to make a fresh start. Amen.

Seeds of a New Year

Early on the morning of January 1, 2023, I wrote the following letter to my family:

The first of a new year. Ripe with potential. Nothing is yet used, wasted nor invested.

In this very moment our dreams and hopes for the year are but tiny seeds, entrusted to us to plant, nurture, and tend—always mindful that in the end, it is God who gives the growth.

Yes, it *is* God who gives the growth, but not without our attention and action. And so, we wonder what will come of these seeds we now hold in our hearts?

Will the tiny seeds of tomorrow one day bear fruit to feed the hungry?

Maybe these seeds are destined to inspire and encourage.

What is the full potential within these seeds—these seeds of tomorrow?

Will we ever know? Or will these seeds that we call "hopes and dreams" be buried alive, left to die?

Beginning today, may we all aspire to be our best selves each day of 2023.

May we willingly do our part—to work hand-in-hand with the Giver of all good gifts—the Source of life itself!

At the end of the year, as 2023 draws to a close, may we hear God whisper, "Well done, good and faithful servant." And as we stand on the threshold of 2024, may these seeds for which we have prayed, and in which we have invested our time and attention, nurtured, and sacrificed, bear witness to God's goodness and our faith in God's faithfulness to let us not labor in vain.

PRAYER

Only you, Lord, know what tomorrow holds. We trust that out of your goodness and love, you will prepare the way, and equip us to meet whatever challenges we will face. With faith in your faithfulness, may we greet every opportunity with willing spirits and grateful hearts. Amen.

Runaway Children of God

The "nones" have been the subject of many conversations within the family of faith over the past decade or two. Some in this group are our own troubled children, who when asked their religious affiliation, respond "none"—hence the name.

I prefer to refer to them as our "runaways." Make no mistake, whether they agree or not, they still belong to the family. They may choose to ignore us, and refuse to claim us, but we are still their family of faith.

We hold fast to our belief in God's unwavering love for all God's children—for all creation. We have faith that, one day, our runaways will return.

Sadly, there are reasons most of them have left the community of faith. Some have been abused. Some are misunderstood. Some have been shunned, and some have chosen to leave in solidarity with brothers and sisters who have suffered the above. Of course, there are also those who have simply drifted away. Now, they are so far from where they started, they're not sure which direction to go to return home even if they wanted.

All runaways may appear lost, but they aren't. They will never be lost. Whether they realize it or not, they rest in God's hands. They remain in our hearts. And certainly, they are in our prayers every day. Because we love them, we honor their dignity to make their own choices, just as

God has given all humanity the gift of freewill. Of course, from the beginning, humanity has exercised this freedom, sometimes in ways that have saddened the Heavenly Father. Nonetheless, the Father never loses sight of any of us, nor does the Father push any of us away. We are always welcome to return home anytime we choose. The same is true for our runaways.

Why do we not chase after them? Because the experience of others has shown that when chased, the faster they run. The better way—the way Jesus proposes through the parable of the "lost son"—is to abide. That means, stay where we are. That means we wait, and while we wait we pray for their safety, an awareness of God's abiding presence with them, the wisdom to know right from wrong, and the courage to choose what is right and pleasing in God's sight.

No doubt, the Heavenly Father is yearning and watching for all the runaways to return. The church, like the unmentioned Mother, faithfully waits alongside the Father. Together they wait and watch. The Father reassures the Mother. The Mother prays without ceasing. Both look forward to the day when the runaways will appear in the distance. Together, without hesitation, they will run to them, and without questions or lectures, embrace their beloved children. Once they appeared lost but are now home! What a day of rejoicing it will be!

PRAYER

With our hope held high, God, we pray with eager anticipation for the day our runaways return. Thank you for the assurance that you continue to hold them in your hand and that your Holy Spirit walks beside them, whether they realize it or not.

Only you know the full story of why they have chosen to leave home. What void may they be trying to fill? What unmet needs do they have? What regrets and resentments are they carrying?

O Heavenly Father, what might we have missed? In what ways have we unintentionally abandoned them—or have we held them so tightly, they've feared suffocation while gasping for breath?

You alone know what is best for them at this time in their lives. We trust that you love them even more than we do, and nothing, absolutely nothing, will be able to separate them from your love that is theirs through your own son, our Lord, in whose name we pray. Amen.

PRAYERS OF THE PEOPLE

"And pray in the Spirit on all occasions with all kinds of prayers and requests. With this in mind, be alert and always keep on praying for all the Lord's people."

EPHESIANS 6:18

The Long Prayer

Confession time: The most dreaded part of the worship service for any child and many adults is "the long prayer," officially referred to in the bulletin as Prayers of the People. It usually comes after the sermon when the congregation is already getting antsy and ready to stand for the final hymn and benediction.

For years, leading the Prayers of the People was one of my primary roles in worship. This meant that the ride home from church usually included having to explain to my young children, one more time, why this prayer had to be so long. In case you've always wondered the same, here's the litany of what is to be included—according to the _Book of Common Worship_: Worldwide and local concerns; the ministry and ministers of the universal church; the nation and those in authority; peace and justice worldwide; the earth and the responsible use of its resources; the community and those who govern it; the poor and oppressed; sick, bereaved and those who recently died; the lonely; all who suffer in body, mind or spirit; and those with special needs. The list alone is longer than most congregants' attention-span.

My favorite story about this prayer is also one of my most uncomfortable moments in worship.

Cliff chose to preach on prayer, using Matthew 6:5-15 as the text. This is the passage about not heaping up empty phrases as the Gentiles, who think they'll be heard because of their many words. It's also the one that talks about hypocrites that love to stand and pray in the synagogues and on street corners. The longer he preached the more emphatic he became and the lower I shrunk down my chair.

By the time I was to take my place in the pulpit to pray, I was dumbfounded. I had a two-page prayer ready to deliver! What was I to say? Standing in the pulpit, I silently looked around the sanctuary, drew a deep breath and asked, "Do you have any idea what it's like to be the one charged with leading 'the long prayer' after a sermon like that?" It was apparent by their laughter that they understood. I also sensed they were thinking they were glad it was me and not them!

So, next time you're in worship and it comes time for the Prayers of the People, please breathe a prayer for the pastor charged with leading it.

PRAYER

Holy, Holy, Holy, Lord God Almighty,

We praise you for the heritage of faith we share with all God's people, and for the promise of everlasting life through Jesus Christ our Lord and Savior. During this time of worship, we pray for ears to hear the alleluias of the saints on high and the heavenly hosts as they continually sing praises to your name. Bolster our faith that we may join our quivering voices with theirs and, for a moment, witness a glimpse of heaven on earth.

We confess that it's so easy to lose sight of your glory when our attention is drawn to earthly concerns. Keenly aware of your love for this fractured world, we take solace as we imagine you cradling it in your arms as we pray for world leaders who hold the reins of power in their hands. May your Holy Spirit give them a shared vision of peace on earth, that will cause them to loosen their grip, put down the reins, and listen to one another with an ear for collaboration and compromise.

We pray for all who are prejudiced and proud of it. Clear their eyes and humble their hearts that they may recognize how distorted and dangerous, callous and cold, bitter and suspicious they have become. Renew a right spirit within them, transforming their rage into a desire for reconciliation with the targets of their wrath.

For the frightened and lonely, the disenchanted and

the distraught, the mentally ill, and the physically impaired, we pray that your healing touch be upon them. For those struggling with addictions, and others who have given up the battle, we ask that you surround them with a network of support offering wise counsel, friendship, honesty, and hope for today. May the joy, love, kindness, and goodness you give us in full measure overflow onto those who need it most. May all we say and do be glorifying to you. We pray this in Christ's name. Amen.

United or Untied

For just a minute, look at the two words, "united" and "untied." They have the exact same letters in almost the same order, with one exception. It's the "i." Depending on where the "i" is placed, the meaning of the word dramatically changes. How easily "united" can become "untied."

Whatever is being described—a family, congregation, organization, or preschool class—can start off as a cohesive group, and by simply moving the letter "i," it falls apart.

In case you've ever felt like your presence or participation doesn't matter, be assured that it does! Remind yourself of this: We are all members of the Body of Christ, and if I am missing or out of place, the Body of Christ is incomplete. The Body goes from being united to fractured when I am not present and involved. I am important to the Body and I want to find my place and do my part to make the Body of Christ complete and whole.

PRAYER

Merciful God, how easily we can move from "united" to "untied" when I am not in the right place. How easily close-knit relationships can unravel because of one dropped stitch.

It only takes one skipped beat to suddenly be out of step, or one wrong turn to be lost. One matters. May I remember to recognize and respect the value of the one standing beside me or sitting behind me. Each one is important.

When I question what difference my presence makes to the Body of Christ, remind me that each and every one of us is important and necessary for the Body to be healthy and whole.

Help me find my place within the Body of Christ—a place where I can unite with others and serve you faithfully. Surrounded by the Body, I am much stronger and more effective than when I attempt to stand alone. Amen.

On Pentecost We Gather

One of my favorite paintings is of Jesus dressed in a robe made of the flags of nations around the world. On Pentecost Sunday I would share this image with the children, making the point that Jesus is Savior of the *world*—not just those of us in the United States.

Even though we speak different languages, dress differently, and have hobbies and interests that are not the same, the one—and most important—gift we share is our faith in Jesus Christ as Lord and Savior of us all. May we never lose sight of our oneness in Christ.

PRAYER

We give thanks for the gift of your Spirit, Lord, that binds us together as members of your global household, inclusive of all who have ever called upon your name and trusted in your faithfulness. What a gift it is to belong!

Expressions of gratitude are offered from all parts of the world today in languages foreign to our ears but certainly known by you. By the power of your Spirit, may we recognize the unique gifts of our brothers and sisters who sing your praises, cry out to you, and pray in ways that differ from our own.

We acknowledge that even people with whom we share a common language may speak in ways we fail to understand. Slow us down, Lord, that we may earnestly listen to the unspoken as well as what is being shared. Sharpen our sensitivity that we may be able to read between the lines of their pain. Give us the ability to comprehend the language of grief in order that we may respond with compassion; the language of despair, so we may respond with encouragement; and the language of the weary and lonely, that will allow us to reach out with comfort and friendship.

We admit that we are guilty of having used words and actions to harm one another. Give us the humility to ask for forgiveness from those we have offended. Erase from our memory the pain we have suffered—pain that is imprinted on our minds—pain that continues to stir resentment and bitterness against those who have wronged us.

Help us be like you, Lord, who knew the pain of betrayal by your closest friends, yet graciously extended forgiveness to them in a single word, "Peace." Only by the transforming power of your Spirit can we so graciously forgive others as you have forgiven us. Amen.

PRAYER

How can we hail you as God of All, yet continue to harbor prejudice and plot harm against any who are different from ourselves? We are divided by geographic borders, political lines in the sand, and even how we interpret your holy word. Forgive us for allowing these differences to take precedence over our loyalty to you. Forgive us when we, like Jonah, are only open to your call if and when it suits us. Amen.

The Lord's Prayer in Everyday Language

When the disciples asked Jesus to teach them to pray, scholars believe he took a prayer from the Jewish tradition and adapted it to be the "Our Father," as it is referred to in some traditions. The prayer as recorded in Luke 11:1-4 (NRSV) varies from the traditional version we pray today, but the essence of it remains. The Lord's Prayer has proven to be timeless and prayed by all denominations and traditions with slight modifications. Many Christians know it by heart. Some of us can say it in our sleep! For this reason, we risk saying it without praying it.

One way to guard against this is to do what I have done: Take time to meditate on it line by line, then attempt to rewrite it in your own words. The following is my version of The Lord's Prayer in everyday language, written in January of 2012.

PRAYER

Our Father who is so beyond us,

Your name is set apart from all others. Your name is revered worldwide.

We long for you to make it obvious that you're the one in charge,

You're the one who calls the shots here on earth just as you do in heaven.

Until then, we ask that you provide us what we need for today.

And please forgive us when we fall short and fail to come through for you—just as we forgive those who do us wrong.

Steer us away from situations and stuff that aren't good for us — that we're weak to resist— and protect us from habitual sins that undermine your plan and bring out the worst in ourselves and others.

We know you can do all of this because all the world is yours. You're the One with all the power, and all credit goes to you now and forever! All of us who are sure of this shout, "So be it!"

Pentecost, Prophets, and Prophesy

"In the last days it will be, God declares, that I will pour out my Spirit upon all flesh, and your sons and your daughters shall prophesy, and your young men shall see visions, and your old men shall dream dreams. Even upon my slaves, both men and women, in those days I will pour out my Spirit; and they shall prophesy... Then everyone who calls on the name of Lord shall be saved." Acts 2:17-18, 21

Are there still prophets in this day and age? Based on this passage from Acts 2, I'd say, absolutely! If so, who would you consider to be a contemporary prophet?

God declares that the Spirit will be poured out upon *all* flesh. Sons and daughters shall prophesy, see visions, and even the old will dream dreams. Slaves, both men and women, will receive God's Spirit and they, too, shall prophesy. Does this mean we are all prophets? It's possible but not probable.

First, prophets never have been fortunetellers, even though it may seem so, when their vision actually comes to fruition. However, rather than foretelling they are what we could call "*forth*tellers," so says Father Richard Rohr, contemporary theologian, contemplative, and author of numerous books. According to Rohr, "forthtellers" are futurists. They have a gift for imagining and seeing the "big picture," or God's ultimate plan for restoring the face of the earth.

The biblical prophets were called and gifted with spiritual insights about the kingdom to come. Prophets were God's mouthpiece—speaking truth to a generation that was often going astray. For this reason, prophets were seldom popular. Their message was tough to take, delivered with boldness, urgency, and passion.

Martin Luther King Jr. was a modern-day prophet. He had a dream—a vision of God's ideal society. With broad brush strokes, and deep, rich colors, he painted a picture of the future with his words—a picture of what could be, and God's plan for what's to come.

With this vivid picture in mind, he then spoke truth to the ills of the present society, and like the prophets of old, his message was not what people in power wanted to hear. His vision was embraced by a wide swath of Americans— men, women, people of color, and whites alike.

From east to west, and north, all the way to the deep south, people were rising up for truth and justice. As his popularity grew, so, too, did his threat to power, and he was eventually assassinated—martyred for his prophetic vision and word.

There are other prophets in our midst. Just look for

them—men and women of courage and conviction who are willing to be persecuted for speaking the truth. Men and women who are standing for justice. Maybe you're one of them?

PRAYER OF THANKSGIVING AND THE LORD'S PRAYER

We give thanks for the gift of your Spirit, Lord. Expressions of gratitude are offered from all parts of the world today in languages foreign to our ears but certainly known by you. We acknowledge that even people with whom we share a common language may speak in ways we fail to understand. Equip us to be able to converse in languages we don't consider ourselves fluent: The language of grief; the language of despair; the language of the weary.

By the power of your Spirit, grant us empathetic ears to hear, and comprehend, the cries for help that are muffled by the proverbial masks behind which we hide.

Verse us in how to ask for forgiveness from those we have hurt. Help us erase the word-pictures that stifle our attempts to forgive those who have wronged us.

On this day of Pentecost, we gather around your table to remember. We remember when you came face to face with your closest friends who had betrayed and deserted you. With a single word, "Peace," you offered forgiveness and sought reconciliation.

We too have turned our back on you, ignoring your presence and thus forfeiting the peace you freely offer. Just as you opened the eyes of those who loved you then, we ask that you open the eyes of those who love you now.

As bread is broken and cup shared, we remember. We remember the night of your arrest and how you took the bread, blessed it, broke it, and invited your disciples to take and eat in remembrance of you.

We remember the grace you poured out as you declared the new covenant sealed in your blood—a covenant of forgiveness for all who call upon your name.

Send your Spirit upon us, and these elements, that they may be the bread of heaven, and the cup of salvation. In the partaking of them, may we be compelled to proclaim the saving grace of your undying love, fully revealed through the death of your only begotten Son until he comes again.

Hear us now—scattered as we are—as we pray aloud in one voice: *Our Father, which art in heaven. Hallowed be thy name. Give us this day our daily bread and forgive us our debts as we forgive our debtors. Lead us not into temptation, but deliver us from evil, for thine is the kingdom, and the power, and the glory forever. Amen.*

Around Christs Table

On Sunday, March 8, 2022, the congregation gathered to receive the Lord's Supper. Heavy on our minds were the thousands of people—mainly women and children—fleeing from Ukraine. Vladmir Putin and Russian troops had invaded the Ukraine. The desperation of Ukrainian President Volodymyr Zelenskyy came across loud and clear as he pleaded with the United States and other countries to come to their aid.

In the neighboring country of Romania, the staff of New Opportunities for Romanian Orphaned Children (NOROC) was at the border with food, supplies, and assistance—including provisions for temporary housing and transportation—as refugees came with nothing more than what they could carry. Because our congregation already had a means of safely sending funds to NOROC, we were confident that every penny given would be used by the NOROC President, Petru Solca, to help these displaced people. The generosity of the church family and the congregations of Palo Duro Presbytery was heartwarming and deeply appreciated. More than $31,000 was given and sent to provide relief. More funds followed from individuals across the presbytery.

The following prayer was offered as we prepared to receive communion, mindful of our oneness in Christ, at such a devastating time in the lives of thousands.

PRAYER

Oh Lord, by faith and with humility, we take our place at your table, aware that your table spans the globe and that at the far end of the table—beyond our sight—there are millions of your children who are also clinging to your promises of faithfulness, forgiveness, and your abiding presence—not as they're seated on padded pews, but fleeing on foot—desperately crying out to you for protection, provisions, for peace.

Here in the quietness of this sanctuary, we pray for all who are seeking sanctuary and for all who are providing it. Acting in your name, may we honor you by holding fast to the spirit of compassion and generosity that can so easily slip through our fingers when we become weary of war, easily distracted by the mundane, and eager to move on to more pleasant matters and means of serving you.

Stir us from complacency by bringing to our conscience our oneness in you—in order that just as we readily rejoice with those who rejoice, may we willingly weep with those who weep.

Please grant leaders around the world the wisdom needed to make decisions that lead to lasting peace. In circumstances that require far more than what is humanly possible, we lean heavily on your sovereignty to exercise your prerogative to carry out your will on earth as it is in heaven.

Around the world and throughout the ages, your people have recognized you in the breaking of bread and drinking from the common cup. May the unity we share as we partake of this sacred meal, be a true reflection of our oneness in you. May we remember our shared story—the story of you—on the night of your arrest when you took the bread, blessed, broke it, and gave to your disciples saying, "This is my body broken for you. Take, eat. Do this in remembrance of me." And, later in the evening, when you took the cup and in the same manner gave to your disciples saying, "This cup is the new covenant sealed in my blood for the forgiveness of sin. Drink all of it."

We ask now that your Spirit be upon us and these elements that the bread we eat and the cup we drink be to us your body and blood, and by the power of this same Spirit, may we be transformed into a truer reflection of you.

And now, as we eat this bread and drink of this cup, we remember you until you come again. It is in your name we pray. Amen.

The following was written in the early '90s, when AIDS was still surrounded by hysteria.

Lay Down My Life?

"…Greater love has on one than this, that he lay down his life for his friends." **John 15: 9-13**

Lay down my life? That's radical, wouldn't you say?
Lay down my life. Is there any other way?
Lay down my life. Are we talking death as in void of
brainwave and breath?
My child, my child, your vision so deem.
I'll show you many ways to die for a friend:
"Mommy, Mommy, come play with me,"
tugging on an arm she wistfully pleas.
Common responses I've heard oft before?
"I'm busy now," and "Don't bother me."
But I say, lay down your life for such as these.
There's so little time and so much to do…
Quiet my child as I'm teaching you.
Think of the lounge and the sounds that one hears:
Sarcasm excused as an innocent joke,
Gossip disguised as genuine concern,
Slander justified by self-righteous folks.
Where are you, o' child of mine?
You flee from this place as if pleasing me!
Stay!

Stay and give voice to those they abuse,

Stand up for their worth as worthless they seem.

Lay down your pride and defend them I plea.

But they'll turn on me and call me a prude...

Quiet, my child, I'm feeding you.

Now out on the streets I want you to go.

The hatred is rampant, and anger abounds.

Prejudice infects society's sores.

Poor snub the rich.

The rich ignore.

People of color fight among themselves.

Whites gloat supremacy as silent they dwell.

Self-righteous brothers spew condemnation on others.

People with AIDS are shunned and feared.

Their bodies wither when itself it abandons.

Following suit, loved ones retreat.

Fathers leave sons and sisters leave brothers.

They leave them to die,

Their own flesh and blood!

Away from the pain,

Away from the shame,

Run, run, run...

Won't you find time to stay awhile?

Lay down your life and comfort these.

Cradle and nurture them with loving arms.

But my stomach turns when I see such pain...

My child, my child, lay it aside.

Don't you hear their cry?

Lay down your life,
I'll bring you my peace.
Now move to the Church,
A safe gentle place.
A haven for sinners and refuge of rest.
But watch your step as you enter these halls,
Many stumble and often fall,
as they busily lay bricks,
to build more and more walls.
Walls to contain and walls to exclude.
Walls to separate the "good" from the "bad."
Beware these walls, I'm warning you.
The bricks they lay are laced with confusion.
Heavy with law, they're a burden to bear.
Remember dear child, I give rest to the weary.
Remember dear child, my love knows no bounds.
There are many, you know,
Who have fled from there.
Feeling inferior and weak with sin,
They see these bricklayers as strong virile men.
Flexing muscles the scriptures they quote.
Picking and choosing the words they will share,
My lame and malnourished lay dying in there.
Where is the balm to soothe their wounds?
Where are the healing hands to brush their brow?
O' child of mine, I know you care.
Gently make windows so my light I may share.
Swing open the doors, and my Spirit I'll send,

Like a breath of fresh air, I promise to come in.

Wait Lord, you don't mean me?

I'm only a woman, too timid to speak.

No Child, I know you.

I formed you in the womb.

Yet, before I formed you, I knew you.

Before you were born, I set you apart.

And for those I foreknew I also predestined to be conformed

in the likeness of my Son.

It's time Child,

Lay down your fears and I'll make you complete.

But...

Did not Christ lay down his life for you?

Is it too much to ask?

Just pause for a while,

Let my Spirit speak.

I'll take your hand and guide your feet.

Together, we'll bring comfort to all those who suffer.

Where there is conflict, we'll serve as the buffer.

Spreading joy and proclaiming peace,

we'll choke out pessimism, that robs all of hope.

Is it too much to ask for love such as this?

Simply, lay down your life for your sisters and brothers.

And Jesus said: *"Greater love has no one than this, that he lay down his life for his friends."*

John 15:13

Storms of Life

In September of 2017 Hurricane Irma hit the coastline of Florida, killing eighty-four people, and causing damages that were estimated at $50 billion. Just a few weeks earlier, Hurricane Harvey slammed the Texas coastline with 130 mph winds. Obviously, the reality of how ferocious nature can be came home to both states that year.

Focusing on the power and presence of God is one way to offer assurance to battered victims. As big and bad as the storms that brew off the coast or in our homes may be, God is mightier, and God will see us through whatever danger we face. On this conviction, we can drop anchor and hold fast.

PRAYER

Almighty God, we come to you this morning with heavy hearts for all who have had their lives turned upside down—either by natural disaster or an unexpected diagnosis. Among our friends and family there are those of us who have recently lost jobs, others who are attempting to piece together the chards of treasured relationships that have shattered. Clinging to the wreckage of our lives, we are desperate for the assurance of your presence, believing that this assurance comes with the strength to hang on and ride out the storm.

As the unrelenting wind continues to wreak havoc, and flood waters overwhelm thousands of homes and businesses, churches, and schools, we yearn to make an authentic response by doing what we can to ease the burden and demonstrate our support for the victims.

We give thanks for Presbyterian Disaster Assistance, and other emergency organizations, that coordinate volunteers who are willing to drop their own lives to be of aid to those in distress. May all be empowered and encouraged to confront the challenges others are facing and, by so doing, make your presence known in tangible ways.

Unrest is prevalent throughout your creation, Lord. Nations continue to assert power and impose control over each other. We ask, Lord, that leaders and those who advise them will seek peace rather than revenge. May all in positions of authority experience the weight of the world on their shoulders, and turn to you with pleas for direction, and solutions. May they have the humility and wisdom to listen to you and to agents of your peace.

Within our own homes and communities, there are chaotic circumstances, misunderstandings, brokenness to which we may have contributed—either directly or indirectly.

As painful as it is to realize our own culpability, open our eyes to see the damage we may have done. Grant us the humility to seek forgiveness from those we have harmed. Freely you have forgiven us, may we in turn, generously forgive one another.

We take comfort in knowing that you brought order from chaos before the earth was formed. Over the eons, you have conquered storms and parted seas to rescue your people. Trusting to see us through all the storms of life, and to never forsake us, we drop anchor and hold fast. Amen.

Global Crisis

For once the entire world feared a common enemy, endured a common struggle, and experienced compassion for strangers as well as those they held most dear. The worldwide pandemic leveled life's playing field and left no one unscathed. All suffered in some way and to some degree and, because it was global, there was nowhere to run—no means of escape.

Ironically, we were all in this together, yet physically apart. Institutions, stores, public facilities were no longer accessible. There was speculation as to the long-term effects this cloistered way of life would have on schools and churches. Would the students and worshippers return? We would have to wait and see.

The following prayer was prepared for Sunday morning worship on August 23, 2020.

PRAYERS OF THE PEOPLE

You alone are sovereign, God, and worthy of praise. For so long sanctuaries of your church around the world have been silent and empty. Your people have been scattered and scared. We long for the day when we can again gather and immerse ourselves in worship of your holy name.

As some of us hesitantly return to the pews, we give thanks for the comfort and assurance we find in your sacred spaces. We acknowledge that your church is not made of brick and mortar but life and breath. We are the church, the community of faith, the body of Christ, joint heirs with Christ. How humbling it is to consider ourselves as Jesus's siblings. Please give us the courage and confidence to live into our identity as your sons and daughters.

There are many for whom we are praying today. Some struggling with physical ailments, others with faltering marriages. Some are finding it hard to get out of bed. The days are long and empty. The house is hollow since loved ones have died or moved away. Some are anxiously attempting to keep a lid on their fears as the "what ifs," haunt them. And then there is the silent majority who suffers in silence.

What a relief it is to know that you know our needs before we ask. Our condition and situations are fully known by you. There is no need to be able to clearly define the source of another's pain—not even our own, nor prescribe the cure. With a sigh of relief, we simply cry out, "Have mercy on us!" You are the Great Physician.

This morning we specifically pray for this fractured nation. Awaken us to the hidden oppression under which so many live due to prejudice, mental illness, poverty, and abuse. Create within us an insatiable hunger for justice. Equip us with the humility to recognize and admit our own culpability when, either out of ignorance or with intentionality, we have caused or perpetuated the pain of our neighbor. Forgive us we pray, and may we have the courage to seek forgiveness from those we have harmed.

As your disciples in this present age, teach us how to love the most offensive among us, and how to forgive those who ridicule and deride us, for by loving and forgiving our enemies, your grace is most fully revealed. Amen.

PRAYERS OF PETITION

"Do not worry about anything, but in everything by prayer and supplication with thanksgiving let your requests be made known to God and the peace of God, which surpasses all understanding, will guard your hearts and your minds in Christ Jesus."

PHILIPPIANS 4:6-7

Thy Will Be Done

Prayers of petition seem to be our strong suit. We are good at asking God for what we want. We lean heavy on words from scripture like, "ask and you shall receive," however, we also know from experience that this isn't always true. So, how do we explain it when we don't get what we want? What do we say when we've prayed healing for someone who died anyway?

Some of us stomp away and swear never to ask God for anything ever again. Others of us begin rationalizing why God didn't answer the prayer as requested, and a few of us shrug our shoulders and admit that we don't know.

I think it is worth noting that even Jesus didn't get what he requested of the Heavenly Father, when he prayed, *"My Father, if it is possible let this cup pass from me; yet not what I want but what you want."* Matthew 26:39 Scripture tells us that he prayed this three times, yet as we know, Jesus was crucified anyway. So, for those who argue that prayers aren't answered due to a lack of faith, this simply isn't always the case.

Note that Jesus stipulates, "Not what I want but what you want," or in other words, "Thy will be done." Only when we are convinced of the goodness of God are we able to honestly pray in this manner. Only when we trust that God's ultimate plan for all creation is born of love are we able to inequitably say, "Have your way with us, Lord."

Think of it from the perspective of a child and parent. There are some things that a child may request that the parent knows are not in the best interest of the child or others. The parent also knows that there is no way of explaining this to the child in words that he or she will understand. The same is true with God. We do not have the ability to see the big picture or know all the ramifications of a single "Yes," to our prayer request. Trusting in God's goodness and God's love of all creation makes it easier to be less insistent on what we request and more confident when praying, "Thy will be done."

The Road to Pulpit, Table, and Font

The following journal entries were not intended for publication, but since the title of this book suggests personal confession, these excerpts from my journal are as intimate as anything I've ever committed to paper. I offer these entries in hopes that someone who is heeding the call to ordained ministry might benefit in some way from receiving a glimpse of my journey.

For clarification: A Master of Divinity degree (M.Div.) usually takes three years of full-time study. I chose to attend seminary part-time for six years.

November 1999

God, this morning I'm so aware of my physical limitations. My ability lags far behind my zeal for learning, achieving, and serving. I'm now almost a year into graduate school and I know without a doubt that I am called to complete the Master of Divinity degree and be ordained as a Minister of Word and Sacrament, but I am so tired. So, what am I to do? Am I to find a way to accelerate the journey to be able to complete the M.Div. quickly and get on with what I am called to do, or am I to continue plodding along at this pace?

The thought of exercise just flashed through my mind. Zipping along to the M.Div. might be like putting my whole self into it. Doing an intense set of jumping jacks. Boldly engaging my entire body in the action. Whereas taking one or two courses a semester while working full-time is more like being flat on my back trying to hold my feet a few inches off the floor. Which is harder? I can answer that in a heartbeat: Holding my feet a few inches off the floor. I've never had the stomach for that! But then, maybe that's exactly what I need to do. Maybe the value of taking the long way through school is to strengthen my patience and perseverance. However, I'm so tired it hurts.

August 2000

Dear God, Am I doing what you would have me do or am I being pushed along by some unhealthy force— driven to impress, please, over-achieve? Is this question the work of evil to discourage and derail me from doing your will or is it of you? It just seems like this mountain is so huge and I don't know if I have what it takes to climb it. I don't want to quit. I want to move up the mountain, but I fear losing it—losing something: my sanity, these precious days and moments of Greg and Julie's lives, Gene, light-heartedness, the ability to get excited about simple things in life. I feel different from other moms who seem to be consumed by their children's activities. Am I selfish—always running my own course, considering my own agenda? I confess that I envy those who appear so content in careers that are second to family and friends—those who work to make enough money to *live* with those they love.

I've almost forgotten what it's like to get excited about making gifts for Christmas, landscaping the backyard, redecorating the house, cooking meals, planning a birthday party. I feel so different and so alone at times. Maybe I need to adopt an event or holiday and throw myself into planning and preparing for it—even if I don't feel like I have the time, energy, or enthusiasm for it.

Help me, Lord. I don't know what to do. How can I do it all: work full-time, go to school part-time, and be an attentive wife and mother? God, you know how to make it work. Please grant me wisdom, courage, energy, enthusiasm, clarity, vision, and whatever else I need for wholeness. Grant me shalom.

June 5, 2001 - Austin Presbyterian Theological Seminary (6-weeks of Greek studies)

I don't know if I can adequately express it, God, but it is a conviction unlike any other that I have ever experienced. What I am called to do is less about me and more about Thee. I'm thankful for the confirmations along the way that serve as reminders that this journey is by design and you are with me. I don't know in what ways you will use what I am studying and learning, or what value the proper credentials will have in opening doors through which to pass in order to do the work you're calling me to do. It's a free-fall of faith and I'm still way too far above the clouds to even imagine where I may land. But for now, I'm simply content and confident that the leap of faith I've taken by embarking on seminary studies is pleasing to you, Lord, and that's enough.

February 2005

This is the final semester. I will soon graduate with the Master of Divinity degree—90 hours of graduate study. I've almost made it! I just wish the last semester allowed for a light load—a course such as spiritual reflection. I find myself longing to devote time to looking back and realizing all that has transpired over the years and how God has faithfully carried me through. God has worked through so many people to offer me encouragement. Through major losses, grief, and transitions, God has helped me hold fast.

Over the past six years, I have experienced a deep level of reliance on God. I have felt God's presence and recognized God's power equipping me to carry on, no matter what adversity or challenges I had to face. Thankfully, my faith has grown tremendously, and therein I have discovered the peace that surpasses all understanding. I have no doubt that God will give me the time, energy, clarity of thought, and perseverance needed to make it through these last assignments and the oral comps. This journey has been far more difficult and draining than I dared imagine, yet I am so very, very grateful for having experienced it.

Note: I graduated from ACU-Graduate School of Theology in May 2005 and was ordained as a Minister of Word and Sacrament in the Presbyterian Church (USA). In 2015 I graduated from Louisville Presbyterian Seminary with a Doctor of Ministry degree, and after serving on staff at First Central Presbyterian Church for twenty-five years, I retired June 1, 2022.

No Fear Tattoo

The mail arrived the day after Christmas 1996. As I shuffled through some bills and a few Christmas cards, I came to a letter from the radiologist. I opened it, sure that it would confirm that the first of my, now annual, tests would show that I had nothing to fear. I was wrong.

I was also shocked. Ironically, three days earlier, I had slapped a temporary "No Fear" tattoo to my forehead and worn it to church as part of the senior high Sunday school lesson I was teaching. Now, here I was, paralyzed by fear and the "what ifs." What if I have cancer? What if this is the beginning of the end?

The following is an excerpt from a journal entry I wrote the day after receiving the news:

"I learned an important lesson during the night as I wrestled with sleep...Quickly after reading the letter, I began praying, weeping, feeling hopeful, and then feeling despair as I thought of other women who were not spared. Why should I be? Then I'd think of the many I know who have overcome or been granted more time and healing. It was a roller coaster afternoon and night."

Prior to going to bed I had prayed that God would use my dreams to prepare me for what was to come. My head had barely hit the pillow when a revelation came to me: I had always had an enthusiasm for teaching and viewed it as a calling, but lately, as the semester had drawn to a close, I had been feeling a hardening of my heart toward everything about it. Now, in light of the letter, that had all changed. Now I was *eager* to continue teaching. I remember pleading, "God, *please* grant me many years to teach or fulfill any role you have for me. Just let me live."

I was surprised by such a dramatic about-face of my attitude. I was seeing all of life from a different perspective. Relationships, work, daily routines—all were enhanced to treasured status. Nothing was to be taken for granted. All were gifts to be received with gratitude and cherished as if at any moment they could be taken from me—which I suddenly realized was absolutely true.

Drifting off to sleep, I remember feeling at peace. I also remember visualizing a calloused knot over my heart that was beginning to soften and change. In this case, the knot represented my hardened attitude toward teaching. It was as if God had taken advantage of this situation to restore my appreciation for teaching. He had renewed my spirit and sense of call. For this I was grateful.

The next morning, while I was still half asleep, these words from scripture clearly came to me, "*Weeping may linger for the night, but joy comes with the morning.*" Immediately I reached for my Bible to look it up. I found it: Psalm 30:5. That's not all I found.

As my eyes scanned from verse 5 to the beginning of the chapter, the often overlooked description above the passage caught my attention. It reads: "Thanksgiving for Recovery from Grave Illness."

To this day, I choose to believe that this was one more reason God led me to Psalm 30. On that morning, when I needed words of assurance, they were provided. Thankfully, a week later these words proved true. It was also true that "joy comes with the morning."

PRAYER

"To you, O Lord, I cried, and to the Lord I made supplication: 'What profit is there in my death, if I go down to the Pit? Will the dust praise you? Will it tell of your faithfulness? Hear, O Lord, and be gracious to me! O, Lord, be my helper!

"You have turned my mourning into dancing; you have taken off my sackcloth and clothed me with joy, so that my soul may praise you and not be silent. O Lord my God, I will give thanks to you forever."

Psalm 30:8-12

Lake Turnover

Just like a lake as it is turning over, families may find themselves undergoing unexpected upheaval. The future is murky and while one might not go so far as to say it stinks, there is a pungent odor about it. The decay that has been buried deep beneath the surface is now suspended in the water, causing it to look dirty. No longer can a family deny that they are in over their heads. They are suffocating—or so it feels.

Thankfully, the winds of change will once again blow! However, most of us don't welcome change, even if we know it's good for us. Lake turnover is also deceivingly good for us. Hydrologist Robert Ladwig of the University of Wisconsin's Center for Limnology explains: "I think of turnover as the lake taking a deep breath as everything is mixed. It's like a fresh start every spring and fall."

Who among us doesn't need a fresh start from time to time? Continuing to hide behind an illusion of control is like attempting to live underwater by holding one's breath. It can't be done for long. The time has come to break through the surface and draw a long overdue breath of renewed life.

PRAYER

Like Peter crying out, "Lord, save me!" we too are frightened that we are going down. We confess that we can't save ourselves. We need you! We pray that we will be able to see your outstretched hand and will drop all pretense and grab hold of you. During this time of upheaval, as our lives are undergoing a turnover, give us the strength to hold fast to you and the faith to believe that the winds of change are creating an opportunity for a fresh start. Amen.

The Darkest Psalm in the Psalter

Unlike most psalms, Psalm 88 does not end on a high note of praise. This is why it is commonly referred to as the darkest psalm of the psalter. This is the psalm quoted by Jesus in the garden prior to his arrest. The fact that is included in scripture is a testimony to God's compassion and acceptance of our honesty—even if it is dark.

A Contemporary Interpretation of Psalm 88

In the dark of night, I cry out to you, Lord, God of my salvation.

I plead with you, "Please pay attention to my cry!"

My soul is weighed down with worry and sorrow.

Obstacles appear as immovable boulders, blocking all rays of hope from my sight.

I'm sinking into despair.

Where are you, Lord?

Your silence is deafening.

Do you hear me?

Have you forgotten me?

Have I been too much of a bother, too pitiful, for you to consider?

Never have I fallen so far. I am in the depths of darkness,

a foreign place.

I'm drowning in despair.

Waves of doubt overwhelm me, knocking me to my knees.

Where are your waves of mercy? I long for them to wash over me!

What am I to make of my situation?

Either you are not all powerful, or you would rescue me.

Either you are not pure goodness, or I would not be in despair.

Either you are not faithful, or I would feel your presence and experience your peace.

Lord, God of my salvation, I have no peace!

My friends and family are no more than strangers to me now.

They are numb to my complaint.

They shun me. I am a stark reminder of how fragile life can be.

Secretly, doubts and fears stir within them as they see me suffer.

Will they, too, be abandoned by you?

Why have you allowed me to sink into this pit of darkness?

I fear I have sunk lower than the grave.

Faint refrains of praise can be heard rising from the grave. Even the dead praise you!

Your wonders continue to be rehearsed by those who have no voice.

Even the dead are in awe of you!

Am I nothing more than mud on the soles of the dead?

Wadded up inside myself, I shrink smaller and smaller.

I am engulfed by silence and darkness.

You may forsake me, Lord, but I refuse to let go of you!

You are my only hope. If I turn from you, I will surely die.

With the last shred of energy, I will grasp for you from the depths.

Every day I will pester you with my incessant plea:

"Oh Lord, God of my salvation, rescue me!"

Choose Whom You Will Serve

If you've ever questioned God's position on intense expressions of complaint, grief, pain, and confusion—even anger—be assured that God can take it. Not only can God handle it, God encourages our uncensored honesty—and that includes feelings that may make some people of faith uncomfortable. We call these expressions of lament and they are prevalent in the Old Testament, with approximately sixty-five of the psalms considered to be psalms of lament.

Lamentations is as, the name suggests, a book of lament.

As an exercise in writing a prayer of lament, I chose to look at a lovely passage in the New Testament for inspiration, noting how far we, as a society, have strayed from God's desired peace.

SCRIPTURE

Finally, beloved, whatever is true, whatever is honorable, whatever is just,

whatever is pure, whatever is pleasing, whatever is commendable, if there is any excellence,

if there is anything worthy of praise, think about these

things.

Keep on doing the things that you have learned and received and heard from me, and seen

in me, and the God of peace will be with you.
Philippians 4:8-9 NRSV

PRAYER

God of our salvation, we are drowning in a vortex of skepticism. Once trusted heralds of truth are accused of spewing lies and tainted news. Fairness is no longer universally understood but influenced by the bias of the one calling the shots.

It seems that the more barbaric the behavior, and repulsive the speech, the more energized the entranced mob becomes. O God, we rightfully claim to be "One Nation Under God," but now we must ask, how far beneath you have we sunk?

In the belly of greed and gluttony, we wallow, obsessing over the wrongs of others, while ignoring the proverbial log in our own eye. Brothers and sisters in Christ have turned their backs on the teachings from their childhood, like, "love your neighbor as yourself," and songs like, "Jesus Loves the Little Children of the World"—songs that point out the inclusive nature of Christ. It seems as if the master of chaos and fear has taken our nation captive!

Only you, God, have the power to save. Only you, Lord, are due our allegiance. When we are confused and enticed by voices and values other than your own, may these words of conviction call us back, *"Choose, this day whom you shall serve... as for me and my household, we will serve the Lord."* Joshua 24:15.

Amen.

The Cry of Hope

Jean Vanier, the founder of the L'Arche communities, describes in his book, *Becoming Human*, a troubling visit he made to the children's ward of a mental health hospital. He refers to the hospital as a "warehouse of human misery," wherein hundreds of children with severe disabilities were lined up on cots. While this sight must have been troubling, what was even more troubling was the deadly silence. Despite the suffering there was no crying. Why? According to Vanier, when children realize that no one will respond to their cries, they eventually stop crying. Crying is evidence of hope. As long as we have hope, we continue to cry out.

Many Christians in this country are led to believe that a sign of great faith is maintaining a positive, cheerful disposition at all times—even when struck by tragedy or faced with death. To openly grieve makes others uncomfortable, so expressions of sorrow are stifled. We certainly keep to ourselves any anger we may feel toward God, or any accusations of God having abandoned us. These, too, we bottle-up for fear of judgment. Ironically, this stance is not supported by scripture.

David rants, begs, and complains to God, not because of a lack of faith but because he trusts fully in God's faithfulness to listen and God's abiding love. Even Jesus brings his grief and sorrow before God. Like those we read of in scripture, God calls us to honestly cry out in pain as well as with praise. Nothing is hidden from God, he already knows our fears and pain, yet as we wrestle with them to find the words that best express what we are thinking or feeling, God often reveals insights about ourselves, or the situation, that we have not realized or recognized until this moment. For many, our greatest awareness of God's presence has been in times of trial and suffering. It's likely that the sincerest prayers we have ever prayed have been interrupted by sobs.

PRAYER

I cry out to you, Lord, with my face buried in the pillow to muffle the sobs. I kneel in the privacy of the shower where my crying cannot be heard over the sound of water beating on my back—where water washes away the tears that stream down my face.

Oh, God, I pray the same prayer several times a day, and get no direction. My hope is waning as I wait and watch for a glimmer of evidence that you've heard my prayers.

Please, Lord, have mercy on me. Let me recognize your presence and therein experience your peace. In you I find rest. Amen.

On the To-Do List of Life

In the time it takes to pause at a stop sign, the following prayer practically wrote itself. Not expecting to be inspired at such an inconvenient moment, I grabbed for any scrap of paper I could find and hurriedly jotted it down as I drove to the church. Yes, that's right: *as* I drove to church.

This was in 1998 and I hadn't been working at the church long, but long enough to figure out that there is no such thing as down-time in ministry. Writing curriculum, planning VBS, preparing children's sermons, leading Wednesday evening activities, recruiting teachers and shepherds for the young ones in our flock, left little time for reflection and none for rest. Oh yes, I was also the mother of two and wife of one. And I loved all that I was doing! That's how it is with workaholics, so I read in a magazine article one afternoon while waiting for the oil in the car to be changed.

I was eager to read the article, thinking that it would confirm my suspicion that my husband was a workaholic. Never did I consider that the workaholic in our family was me! According to the article and contrary to popular belief, workaholics are not usually martyrs who consider work their master. Most are enthused, motivated individuals who have a passion for what they do, so it makes sense that they tend to take on more and more until one day their health starts to suffer, relationships become strained, or they burn out.

I suffered from the first. Thinking I might be having a heart attack, I was admitted to the hospital for tests. Thankfully, my heart proved good. The diagnosis was extreme fatigue. My body was saying, "No more!" The doctor's orders were for me to take two weeks off and do absolutely nothing but sleep and eat. This may sound inviting to some, but for a workaholic, this is extremely stressful.

One day my co-worker, Cliff, called and shared some research he thought I would find interesting. The study revealed that kangaroos forced to walk on a slow-moving treadmill showed greater signs of physical stress than when allowed to vigorously hop at their normal rate of speed. I think this was Cliff's way of empathizing with me and it worked! What a relief. Someone understood. I am a kangaroo! Did I learn anything else? Yes. I learned how to keep hopping by listening to my body and taking breaks. Thank you,
Cliff!

PRAYER

On the To-Do List of Life,

May I always skip lines.

Remind me, God, of your plans in mind.

Like a wee child with a giant permanent marker,

Wielding my will to and fro,

The risk of damage increases the faster I go.

Grow me up, God, in your grace.

Teach me how to draw and trace.

Draw on you for all direction.

Trace your ways with clear perfection.

Grant me courage to simply give in.

Lay down the marker or colored pen.

Swap for a pencil, eraser intact.

Remove, reword, reroute my day.

Pencil in your work and way.

On the To-Do List of Life

May I always skip lines.

Take my list and make it thine.

Learning to Listen

I have always prayed, but until I was in my late twenties, I considered prayer one-way communication. I was the one praying and God was the one listening. I truly believed that while on this earth I would do the talking and then someday, when seated at the throne of glory, God would speak to me. So, once I had made my requests known, I would say "Amen," and off I'd go to do what I decided was best. As an adult, I would ask for guidance, but never consciously watch for direction. When what I prayed would come to pass, I'd say "God answered my prayers." Requests that didn't get fulfilled were simply referred to as "unanswered."

I was content with this arrangement until so many of my "big ticket" requests had been "answered," and instead of being filled with gratitude I was still wanting for more. I felt like a spoiled child. Here, God had given me all I had asked for and I still wasn't satisfied.

I felt guilty and undeserving of having any more prayers answered—at least for a long time. This is when I decided to make some rules for my prayers. First rule, I could not ask for anything for myself. Part of my refusal to ask for anything, was that I was tired of getting what I requested, and then later feeling like it wasn't enough. I interpreted this to mean that I had asked for the wrong thing—even though at the time I thought God and I were on the same page. The only requests I could make were on behalf of others.

Second rule, every day as I walked around the two-block boulevard where we lived, one full lap was to be devoted to expressing gratitude. My rationale was that I needed to make sure God knew that *I* knew just how blessed I was. A third rule was a revelation born out of a spiritual temper tantrum—metaphorically stomping my feet and shaking my finger at God. I was tired of just guessing what it was God wanted me to do. I wanted answers! Then it occurred to me: If I wanted answers, I needed to be willing to listen. This meant adding a third rule and an extra lap around the boulevard. This lap would be devoted entirely to intentionally listening for God, and not allowing my mind to wander. I wasn't sure if, or how, God would speak, but I knew that I was no longer willing to be the only one doing the talking.

Listening included paying attention to any thoughts or ideas that came to mind—provided they were related to the direction of my life. With God all is possible, so nothing was to be dismissed immediately, but explored as potential options. Immediate answers were not forthcoming; however, I was becoming keenly aware of my surroundings, the people I ran into during the day, and what was going on at the time—aware that God's direction could come through any of these. I was learning to listen with anticipation, and it was making me more alert and aware of life around me. *Expecting* to hear God proved to be the key, since anticipation is evidence of faith!

I have found that God speaks in many ways to trigger our imaginations, rekindle memories, shine a spotlight on priorities, and inspire us to think beyond ourselves. I have also found that there are numerous spiritual practices that have helped God's people connect with the Creator and there are numerous resources on the topic. One of my favorites is a book by Marjorie J. Thompson, *Soul Feast: An Invitation to the Christian Spiritual Life.*

Whatever spiritual practices resonate with you, know that listening—with anticipation of a response from God—will be a key component as you seek to discern God's will.

PRAYER

Sometimes the circuitous path we travel while on this earth may not appear to make sense, Lord. We get discouraged, impatient, and frustrated, when we sense that we have veered off course, or, discovered that we've just been running in circles. Assure us, Lord, that you are always with us, and give us the faith to live with anticipation, trusting that you are eager to guide our steps. Speak, Lord, your children are listening. Amen.

Caught in a Storm

Matthew 14:22-33

"A day like any other day…" these words mark the beginning of the C1 exhibit in the Oklahoma City National Memorial & Museum—an exhibit that walks visitors through the day of April 19, 1995, the day of the deadliest incident of *domestic* terrorism in US history.

On that day, 168 people died, 19 of them being young children who had come to work with their parents that morning to spend the day in the onsite childcare center of the Alfred P. Murrah Federal Building in downtown Oklahoma City.

In addition to the deaths, another 680 were injured by the explosion. One-third of the federal building was also destroyed, as well as 324 buildings within a sixteen-block radius. The estimated cost of damages was more than 652 million dollars.

Viewers of the exhibit are pulled into the reenactment of the infamous day by pictures and sounds. A day that began as any other day: Bacon frying, children brushing their teeth, a woman talking on the phone, the morning weather report. The clock on the wall of the exhibit reads 6:30 a.m. By 9:02 a.m. this day became a day like no other. No one could have predicted the storm that was rolling into town in the back of a Ryder truck.

Whether disasters are attributed to premeditated evil or declared "acts of nature," the storms of life demand a response. Even the threat of a storm, looming overhead, can prove disruptive and drive us to our knees in hopes of warding off the inevitable.

How do you respond when swept up in the chaos brought about by an unexpected, and possibly unprecedented, storm of life?

According to Rebecca Solnit, writer, historian, and activist, "...the image of the selfish, panicky, or regressively savage human being in times of disaster has little truth to it." Solnit bases this claim on decades of meticulous sociological research on behavior in disasters—from the bombings of World War II to floods, tornadoes, earthquakes, and storms, across the continent, and around the world.

In her book, *A Paradise Built in Hell: The extraordinary communities that arise in disaster*, Solnit writes, "In the wake of an earthquake, a bombing, or a major storm, most people are altruistic, urgently engaged in caring for themselves and those around them, strangers and neighbors as well as friends and loved ones."

This is refreshing to hear: Compassion may have the upper hand in a crisis!

When storms strike, the Body of Christ is called to attention, and equipped by the Holy Spirit with the strength, energy, empathy, and faith in God's faithfulness, to fan the flame of hope in those who are struggling to keep their heads above water.

As Christ immediately extended his hand to Peter, who was afraid and beginning to sink, we, the Church— the Body of Christ—are called to reach out to our brothers and sisters in distress. We are also called to vigilantly keep an eye out for any who have slipped through the cracks and are desperately in need of a helping hand.

May we follow the example of Christ and make the first move. With compassion and confidence, may we be willing to walk on water, if necessary, to help those who are caught in a storm. May they, in turn, trust us enough to grab hold of the extended hand of the Body of Christ, giving the church the opportunity to be the church.

PRAYER

O Lord, you are our protector in this stormy world.

When we are paralyzed by fear, give us eyes to recognize you, coming to us through the storm. As weak and hopeless as we may feel, give us the courage to cry out to you, followed by the faith to watch for, and accept, the lifeline thrown our way.

Once back in our proverbial boat, feeling safe and secure, it's tempting to allow the peaceful waters to lull us to sleep. Awaken us!

Prompt us to rub the sleep from our eyes, and look beyond the bow of our own boat, for any whose vessel has capsized and whose faith is frazzled. Empower us to be able to meet their need and pull them into our boat, where they may find rest for their souls and renewed hope for tomorrow. Amen.

Leading from Behind

It was a risky move when God entrusted us with making our own decisions and charting our own course. Allowing humanity to have a say and some degree of control in future outcomes is evidence of God's desire for a relationship rather than a dictatorship. It is also evidence of God's preference for leading from behind.

In his autobiography, Nelson Mandela equates a great leader with a shepherd, explaining that the shepherd walks behind the flock, allowing the nimblest of the flock to take the lead. From behind, the shepherd's eye is always on the flock, while also watching for potential danger. If spotted, the course can be altered, or the flock warned and prepared to confront the threat.

Certainly, leading from behind requires relinquishing some of the control. Not all leaders are willing to step back and share the responsibility of decision-making. It's also true that not all followers are eager to assume the risks associated with leadership. It's easier to mindlessly follow the leader and bear no responsibility if the flock goes astray. However, even though it may be easier in the beginning to blindly follow, it can prove fatal in the end—like sheep being led to slaughter.

In a national vote by German Protestants in July 1933 two-thirds of Christian Protestants supported the leadership of the German Christian Movement. It was this leadership that made significant changes to German Protestantism in an effort to bring it in line with Nazi racial ideology. One change meant that instead of classifying people as Christians or Jews based on their faith, German Christians chose to follow the lead of the Nazi party and classify people by racial heritage. Therefore, church leaders whose parents or grandparents had converted from Judaism to Christianity were considered Jewish and some non-Aryan clergy were forced out of ministry to show support of the regime. By January of 1934, leaders of the German Christian Movement went so far as to vow to purge Protestant churches of all "Jewish influence," including removal of the Old Testament from the Bible.

A propaganda poster that appeared about this same time featured a drawing of Martin Luther and a swastika. It read, "Hitler's fight and Luther's teachings are the best defense for the German people." The German Christian Movement sincerely believed that their loyalty to the popular, charismatic politician, Adolf Hitler, was surely pleasing in God's sight. But as history would reveal, they had been duped and ultimately culpable of wrongdoing.

Perhaps one lesson we can learn from this atrocity is to look for leaders willing to share responsibility for decisions by leading from behind, and to beware of those who insist on hoarding control.

PRAYER

Chief Shepherd of our souls, we rely on the promise of your abiding presence, leading us from behind as we make our way along life's journey. Increase our sensitivity to your nudge as you prod us to step out in faith. Remind us to stick together as a flock, and to be alert to what's ahead. Awaken us to the danger of wolves masquerading as shepherds by attuning our ears to your voice as we listen for your lead at every turn and crossroad.

Spur us on to serve as faithful leaders. Equip us to serve as mentors who demonstrate what it is to live with integrity for your glory. Like those who have gone before us, may we continually be honing our ability to discern your will and walk in your ways. May the joy and peace of being your disciples shine through our lives in order that others may seek to serve as your followers of today and leaders of tomorrow. Amen

The Parable of the Missing Puzzle Piece

Upstairs on one wall we have hanging a framed 999-piece jigsaw puzzle. Before we took it out of the box and started putting it together, it had 1000 pieces. Sometime between removing the cellophane and realizing there was a hole in the landscape, one piece went missing. I have no idea what happened to it. We don't have a dog to blame for eating it, and our granddaughter had not yet been born. It just disappeared. That happens. What were we to do?

I know what Jesus would do. He would look for it, just like the story he told about the woman searching for the lost coin, the shepherd looking for the lost sheep, and the father who never gave up on the lost son. But this is a puzzle piece and, as is true of most predicaments in life, there is more than one suitable solution: First, we could fall to your knees and search for it; second, we could declare the puzzle useless and toss it; third, we could tear it apart, box it up and either stick it back in the cabinet or set it aside for the next garage sale. Whether saved to work again or traded for a dollar-twenty-five, the right thing to do would be to disclose the truth: It's missing a piece.

We opted out of all the above.

We chose to follow through with our original plan: Glue it, frame it, and hang it. What about the blank space? It has since been assigned meaning. That's what we do, isn't it? We figure out a way to make sense of what's gone wrong or what's missing. In this case, the blank space serves as a reminder that more times than not, someone or something will be missing. Seldom does everything go as planned. Rather than assigning all significance and worth to the one missing piece, we chose to recognize the beauty of the 999 pieces we still had.

Would we have preferred to have the missing piece? Absolutely! However, this wasn't the case. So, we made do with what we had and celebrated anyway!

PRAYER

When will we stop expecting life to be perfect, Lord?

Something or someone will always be missing, and all plans are up for revision.

When our grip is so tight that we begin squeezing the joy right out of all we hold dear, remind us to loosen up! Teach us to hold life lightly on open palms.

When we are discouraged and downcast because our plans are not going the way we had hoped, lift our drooping heads, wipe away our tears, and encourage us to open our eyes and behold all the beauty that surrounds us. Encourage us to shift our attention from what is missing to what remains. Inspire us with possibilities and give us a vision of plan B. Bolster our faith to trust in your unchanging faithfulness as we continue to struggle with life's uncertainties. Amen.

A Wild Goose: Raucous and Uncontrollable

A little research verifies that it really is true that the fifth century Christians of the Islands of Britain adopted the Wild Goose as a symbol of the Holy Spirit, preferring it to the serene dove traditionally associated with the Great Divine. Fascinating!

Why would they choose a honking, raucous, uncontrollable fowl over a cooing, calm, and gentle dove? Perhaps because of what we know of the Holy Spirit from scripture.

We read in John 3:8-9 that the Spirit will blow where it will, and there are numerous accounts of miracles that testify to God's Spirit as the behind the scenes force empowering people to part waves, move mountains, heal the blind and lame, and even raise the dead!

In Acts 2, the Holy Spirit comes upon all gathered in a bold way: A violent wind, tongues of fire, and out of control behavior by the disciples, who were accused of drunkenness at nine o'clock in the morning!

The Holy Spirit: Powerful, untamed, unrestrained, blowing, and going where it will, like a magnificent, free bird in flight. Perhaps the Celts were on to something. But a wild goose?

PRAYER

You come to us in the wind and fire, with the potential to both energize and destroy.

You speak to us in the silence and faint tones like the cooing of a dove.

We strain to hear you as we pray for your gentle guidance.

Other times you startle us with the raucous honking of a wild goose, jarring us awake, calling us to action, and warning us of danger.

With both anticipation and hesitation, we listen for your call.

Only by the will and power of your Holy Spirit do we have ears to hear. Amen.

On the Wings of the Wild Goose

Do you ever question whether you're doing enough, or if what you are doing really matters?

Mother Teresa is known for making the point that it's not about doing great works of love but doing even the smallest tasks with great love. She obviously understood that God has the power to use what little we offer in a mighty way. It might be as simple as a smile, a band-aid, a hot biscuit, a can of beans, or a helping hand. Whatever we offer, when given with a positive attitude, God can magnify and multiply to assure both recipients and us of God's love.

Do you ever feel like you're on a wild goose chase—no idea where you're going and certainly no idea as to why?

When I learned that the Celtic Christians in the Fifth Century adopted the Wild Goose as its symbol for the Holy Spirit, it called into question the way I had always interpreted the phrase, "wild goose chase." No longer was its use restricted to folly or being sent on a senseless errand. Now, it could also be understood as a mission divinely directed! The next time you feel like you're on a wild goose chase, trust and pray that you *are*!

PRAYER

God of Surprises, God of Power, prepare us to take flight. Prompt us to be ready to jump and run when you call. Encourage us to eagerly embark on the next "Wild Goose chase!" Remind us that any mission for you—no matter how trivial it may seem—is worthy of our effort, and who knows where it might lead! Grant us the courage and a sense of adventure to accept your call on the wings of the Wild Goose! Amen.

Wild Goose Chase

It was the final worship service of the 2005 Mo-Ranch Women's Conference and keynote speaker Rev. Susan Andrews shared that the Wild Goose was adopted by the Celts centuries ago to serve as the symbol of the Holy Spirit. This being noted, she then offered the following benediction: "And now, may the Wild Goose of God nip at your heels as you go forth from this place!"

The image of a wild goose nipping at my heels brought to mind an expression I'd heard all my life, but never in regard to God. Could it be that the expression, "a wild goose chase," originated in Scotland and originally referred to a positive, productive, and purposeful adventure rooted in the faith? If so, the connotation of "a wild goose chase" that I grew up hearing had certainly gone astray.

Fascinated by this image for the Holy Spirit, I was inspired to create a sermon series that I came to call "A Wild Goose Chase through Ordinary Time." The following story was shared at the close of the first sermon in the series as a fitting example of a "wild goose chase." This story is a family favorite. Some say it's about Uncle Pinto while others claim it's about the former owner of a local funeral home where he once worked. Nonetheless, it's a good story and since I heard it happened to Uncle

Pinto, that's the way I'm going to tell it.

As the story goes, a certain man we'll call "Mr. Smith" died and his funeral was in Abilene. The burial was to be in a neighboring small town where Mr. Smith had been born and reared. After the funeral a long procession of cars followed the hearse bearing Mr. Smith and driven by Uncle Pinto. Arriving on the outskirts of the small town, it dawned on Uncle Pinto that he had no idea where the cemetery was located. Keep in mind that this was long before cell phones or GPS.

Not knowing what to do, Uncle Pinto—with the string of cars on his tail—drove on into town. He took first one turn and then another. He passed the schoolhouse, through downtown, over the railroad tracks, and up and down residential streets in search of the cemetery. As you can imagine, by the time he finally came upon the cemetery he was fit to be tied. He was so sure that the family would be quite upset with him for leading them on what we'd call a "wild goose chase!"

However, as he emerged from the hearse, he saw Mr. Smith's widow hastily making her way to him. He could see the tears in her eyes. The first words she spoke surprised him: "Thank you so much!" Uncle Pinto was confused but tried not to show it. She continued, "My husband would have been so grateful for the time you took to drive him through town and past all the places that meant so much to him." He was stunned. She added, "Especially for driving him by the old homeplace one last time."

Sometimes we just don't know when, where, or why the Wild Goose of God is leading us in a particular direction, but be assured, God is working through us whether we realize it or not!

BENEDICTION

Like the honking of a wild goose, may the Lord relentlessly bother and challenge you. Nipping at your heels, may the Wild Goose of God prompt, prod, and nudge you beyond your comfort zone until you finally choose to follow wherever the Wild Goose is leading. Then and only then, may the Lord grant you peace in the name of the Father, Son, and Holy Spirit. Amen.

BLESSINGS AND BENEDICTIONS

*"Now to him who by the power at work within us is
able to accomplish abundantly far more than all we
can ask or imagine, to him be glory in the church
and in Christ Jesus to all generations,
forever and ever. Amen."*

EPHESIANS 3:20-21

Blessings and Benedictions

A blessing is a declaration or petition for divine favor, such as the beatitudes spoken by Jesus at the beginning of what has come to be known as the Sermon on the Mount, which is a compilation of Jesus's teachings beginning with Matthew 5.

"Blessed are the poor in spirit, for theirs is the kingdom of heaven.

Blessed are those who mourn, for they will be comforted.

Blessed are the meek, for they will inherit the earth.

Blessed are those who hunger and thirst for righteousness, for they will be filled.

Blessed are the merciful, for they will receive mercy.

Blessed are the pure in heart, for they will see God.

Blessed are the peacemakers, for they will be called children of God.

Blessed are those who are persecuted for righteousness' sake, for theirs is the kingdom of heaven.

Blessed are you when people revile you and persecute you and utter all kinds of evil against you falsely, on my account. Rejoice and be glad, for your reward is great in heaven, for in the same way they persecuted the prophets who were before you."

A benediction is a blessing conveyed at the close of a letter or worship service—a parting word of favor. Flip to the final verses of any letters in the New Testament and you will find a brief word of blessing. Paul commonly concludes his letters with "Grace be with you," or "The grace of the Lord Jesus Christ be with your spirit."

Pronouncements of blessing are a beautiful way to reaffirm God's goodness and provision for God's people. May the following blessings and benedictions inspire, empower, and encourage you as you continue the journey.

Bless the Children

When Greg and Julia were young children, one of my favorite rituals—either at night or early in the morning—was to go into their bedrooms while they were sleeping, gently place my hand on their heads, and softly whisper "Aaron's Blessing" over them. I did this for a number of years.

When Greg was in high school, I felt a strong urge to tweak a line from the Lord's Prayer and insert it as the fourth and final line—just before "Now and forevermore." I added, "And may the Lord lead you not into temptation but deliver you from evil." From then on I prayed this over both children.

Only naïve parents think they know everything that's going on in their children's lives—especially once they are teenagers and have the ability and freedom to drive themselves where they want to go. I taught middle school and high school for nine years, and my colleagues and I were aware of far more—maybe not more, but different—details of their teenagers' lives. When parents would protest some accusation about their child by saying, "She would *never* do that!" or "I know my son and there is *no way*, he would…" It's true that we know our children probably better than anyone, but it doesn't mean we know everything that's going on in their lives.

It's also true that while parents continue to have a great deal of influence over their children's choices, once they are adolescents, the opinion and pressure from peers often take precedence. I say this for the benefit of parents who continue to blame themselves for the actions of their children. Granted, parents may have contributed to their teen's poor choices, but it's arrogant to take full responsibility. Face it: At some point, we don't have nearly as much influence as we might think or want to believe.

I have known for many years that as much as I love Greg and Julia, God loves them more. As much as I might think I know what is best for them, I probably don't. But God does.

Standing over them while they were sleeping, with my hand on their heads, and softly offering a blessing was something I could do—for them and for me.

AARON'S BLESSING

Numbers 6:22

May the Lord bless you and keep you,

May the Lord make his face to shine upon you and be gracious to you,

May the Lord lift up his countenance upon you and give you peace,

And may the Lord lead you not into temptation, but deliver you from evil,*

Now and forevermore. Amen.

The Connectional Church

Being part of a denomination that is connectional provides a microcosm of the Body of Christ. We differ from coast to coast and border to border, yet we celebrate our common bond of unity in Christ.

We rejoice in our diversity. We're thankful we're not cookie-cutter copies of each other, that when we gather around the Lord's table, we represent a variety of thoughts, theological positions, life experiences, passions, and causes to which we are called.

As the connectional church, we can join hands and reach around the world. Uniting our voices, we can call for justice, proclaim the good news, and encourage those in crisis around the world.

Together we can make a difference that, individually, we could not achieve.

I'm grateful to be part of the connectional church, where I can learn how to live and serve side-by-side yet not always see eye-to-eye.

BENEDICTION

We have gathered from north, south, east, and west to celebrate life together as God's people. Here in the company of one another, we have been reclaimed, refreshed, reminded of who we are and to whom we belong.

In the breaking of bread and sharing of the cup, we have been reminded that we are not alone. What a blessing it is to be part of the community of faith—the Body of Christ.

As we go forth from this place, let us take a full measure of the love, peace, and joy, we've experienced here today.

Generously, let us share what we've been given with those who need it most.

Let us share it in the name of the Father, Son, and Holy Spirit. Amen.

Hallmark of Christ's Church

In a mobile and fast-paced society—wherein biological bonds are often stretched across the miles; marriages snap under pressure; and families splinter in all directions for a variety of reasons—the church is in a unique position as the household of God to swing open the doors and welcome all to experience the hospitality of Jesus Christ as expressed in and through the Body of Christ. By so doing, the emotional support and sense of belonging that were once primarily fulfilled by the family of origin can be extended and experienced through the family of God.

In the early centuries of the church's life, Tertullian wrote: "It is our care for the helpless, our practice of loving kindness, that brands us in the eyes of many of our opponents. 'Only look,' they say, 'look how they love one another...Look how they are prepared to die for one another.'"

BENEDICTION

May God's legacy of love continue to be the hallmark of Christ's church, and may the lost and lonely in this world be led to the doorstep of our Father's house where we, the church, have the privilege of receiving them with open arms into the household of God, in the name of the Father, Son, and the Holy Spirit. Amen.

Down to Earth God Benedictions

The following benedictions have been written for the seasons of Advent and Christmas.

I did an Advent sermon series that I called "Down to Earth God," recognizing that Jesus is the incarnation of God and was sent by God to live among us on earth and usher in the new age.

ADVENT BENEDICTION

Today we can almost hear the angels sing as we lean into Christmas!

Today we celebrate the purest form of love the world has ever known—a love far greater than we could ever hope to earn.

By the grace of God, we receive this love not on merit, but as a gift from the One whose birth we celebrate.

What more appropriate response might we offer than to model our lives after God's only begotten Son?

By so doing, let us repeat the sounding joy—again and again, day after day!

Let us share the good news:

A Savior is born!

Christ has come!

Christ shall come again!

In the name of the Father, Son, and Holy Spirit! Amen.

CHRISTMAS DAY BENEDICTION

Today is a day of celebration!

Today we celebrate our down-to-earth God, sent by the Heavenly Father.

We celebrate our down-to-earth God, who knew better than to ever leave us alone again. So, together with God, sent the Holy Spirit to abide with us until Christ comes again.

In the meantime, the great Three-in-One sends us, the church, to re-present Christ to the world in this present age, to share the good news, and to bear the Light into the darkened corners of this world. This being said, go!

Go into the neighborhood, your homes, your school, the workplace, the park, and the grocery store!

Go with great joy!

Go and be the church!

In the name of the Father, Son, and Holy Spirit. Amen.

SUNDAYS OF CHRISTMAS BENEDICTION

Mighty Counselor, Prince of Peace, Emmanuel,

Once the tree is removed from the corner of the room, and the lights no longer brighten our doorway...

Once the figurines of the nativity scene are wrapped in tissue paper and returned to their resting place for another year...

Once the halos of angels, and shepherds' crooks are packed and put away...

And once the carols of Christmas no longer fill the air...

May we, your people, continue to proclaim the good news in word and deed:

Christ has come!

Christ will come again! Amen.

BENEDICTION TO PONDER

Just as Mary, mother of Jesus, treasured the words of shepherds, and pondered them in her heart, may we, too, treasure and ponder words that lead to life—words that are honorable, just, pure, pleasing, and commendable.

May each of us in Christ's name, ponder anything worthy of praise, and by so doing, may the peace of God abide in you richly now and forevermore. Amen.

Disciple of Jonah or Jesus?

The last words recorded in the book of Jonah are God's words. God poses a question to Jonah, who is none too pleased that his arch enemies are now among God's people. God asks: *"And should I not be concerned about Nineveh, that great city, in which there are more than a hundred and twenty thousand persons who do not know their right hand from their left, and also many animals?"* Jonah 4:11

That's it. End of story. We have no idea how Jonah responds, which is contrary to the storybook ending we tell our children wherein Jonah accepts the Ninevites. He and God are back on good terms, and everyone lives happily ever after. I think it's far more likely that Jonah stayed miffed at God for saving the arch enemy of Israel. Chances are good that Jonah never set foot in Nineveh again. And it's unlikely that he mentioned to his friends back home his role in God's redemption of the Ninevites. He'd rather die than have done that!

However, to deny the possibility of Jonah having an epiphany and change of heart, is to question God's power to transform prejudice, prideful, rebellious, and resentful prophets like Jonah and people like us into grateful, forgiving, obedient, and dedicated children of God, who rejoice and celebrate when others are welcomed into God's household—even when they are—or were—our worst enemies.

What about you? How do you feel about God's wide-open, all-inclusive hospitality? Are you a disciple of Jonah or of Jesus?

BENEDICTION

Sadly, Jonah would be a popular prophet in our nation today. He could feel right at home on either side of the great divide in our country. But keep in mind, Jonah is not the hero of his own story, nor is he a prophet we are called to emulate. Jonah is, however, a fine example of God's power and faithfulness to carry out the Masterplan of reconciliation with all creation through anyone God chooses to call—as reluctant or rebellious as they may be.

Now, receive the benediction:

Only by God's grace, extended to us through Jesus Christ, do we have hope for a day when all God's people will come together as friends rather than foes, and words of compassion will replace complaint.

In the meantime, consider yourself called to be the good news of Christ's open-arm-all-inclusive hospitality — open and welcoming of all God sends your way — including those deemed the least and the worst, and do so in the name of the Father, Son, and Holy Spirit.

You Go Nowhere Alone

One of my favorite benedictions was written by Rev. Dr. Richard C. Halverson, Chaplain to the United States Senate from 1981 until his retirement in 1995. The original benediction is available online on several websites by searching, "You go nowhere by accident..." I commend it to you.

The following is my adaptation of Halverson's benediction in order that it more accurately reflect my personal theology.

You go nowhere alone.

Wherever you go, God prepares the way.

Wherever you are, God is.

Christ's Spirit, that indwells you,

has something to be done through you,

where you are.

Believe this and go in peace...

Live in Christ's grace...

Share God's love...

Trust in the power of the Father, Son, and Holy Spirit.

AFFIRMATIONS

I affirm that God is always present wherever we are—wherever we go.

I also affirm that God has given humanity the freedom to make choices, some of which may not be in accordance with God's will. Nonetheless, God is with us.

Wherever we choose to go, God has the power and will to prepare the way—maybe not as we would prefer, but in ways that will ultimately play into God's overarching plan for the renewal of all creation.

I affirm that wherever we are, Christ's Spirit is with us and has the power and will to work through us to bring about that which is pleasing in God's sight.

Christ's Spirit continues to equip us to participate in the work God is doing in the world.

Believing this to be true, may we be at peace, assured of the grace extended to us through Jesus the Christ.

Out of gratitude and in response to all God has done, is doing, and will continue to do in the world, we are called to share God's love—confident that the Triune God empowers us to bring glory to God's name in all we say and do. Amen.

Living in Overdrive

If you're not acquainted with Kate Bowler, get to know her through her podcast, "Everything Happens. With Kate Bowler" Aside from the interesting guests she interviews, each episode ends with a blessing—a blessing that is unique in form, and always candidly honest. The following blessing is inspired by her style:

BLESSING

Blessed are you, who power through every day in overdrive...

who, even when your body is at rest, your mind is racing...

for whom yesterday is little more than a blur once you finally steal a glance in the rear-view mirror...

Blessed are you, who add tasks to your to-do list in rapid-fire succession...

who run circles around yourself from dawn until deep into the night...

who are spinning on a stationary cycle, chasing a virtual destination....

whose self-fulfilling anxiety is going nowhere...

Blessed are you, who fear you've lost your breath—

the breath within—the breath of the Spirit that offers refreshment and rest...

May you, exhausted one, slow down and listen for the still small voice within...

May its message come through loud and clear: There is a better way!

May you have the courage to be still and know the God who loves you simply because you are—not because of what you do...

With this assurance, may the peace of Christ wash over you and bring you rest, now and forevermore. Amen.

After the Storm

Whether the storm has been of nature or of our own making, the damage to lives can be devastating. In times like these, the Body of Christ has the opportunity and the responsibility to stand with those who are suffering. The following benediction is a call to the church to be the church.

BENEDICTION

Even though the waters have subsided, the storm rages on in the lives of those who have been uprooted and tossed about in recent weeks.

As the Body of Christ in this present age, we continue to hear Christ calling to us from the turbulent sea—in the dark of night: "Come."

Come with your sleeves rolled up.

Come offering words of encouragement.

Come offering compassion today and hope for tomorrow.

May we, as the Body of Christ, have the courage to step out of the boat,

to wade the waters of change and stand against the current of despair.

May we do so in the name of the Father, Son, and Holy Spirit. Amen.

Do the Hokey Pokey

One of my favorite sermon series was inspired by a tee-shirt. On the shirt was printed, "Hokey Pokey Anonymous," followed by the words, "A place to turn yourself around." I bought it immediately and I continue to wear it—twenty years later!

As a child I loved doing the Hokey Pokey dance. I know now that this precious little dance wasn't written with VBS and children in mind—not at all. It was written for ski bunnies and bums who tumbled into a ski pub somewhere in Idaho back in the '50s! Once the song and dance caught on, and its popularity spread, a guy over in England claimed that he had created the dance, and written the jingle to go with it, back during WWII for the service men and women. The big difference was that his version was called Cokey-Cokey. No surprise, a lawsuit ensued, and I don't recall who won or how it turned out, but the Hokey Pokey survived.

For me, this little song and dance now represent sin and repentance. Repentance actually means to turn around—to go in a different direction—and this is a good thing. Rather than approaching repentance with reluctance, it's time we embrace and receive it as the hope-filled, peace-producing gift that it is: A gift of God for the people of

God, a gift that warrants a positive response from those of us who trust in God's power to redeem and make new. Repentance is a gift that is worthy of our enthusiasm—something worth singing about—as we engage in the process of "turning our lives around." There's no time like the present to do the Hokey Pokey!

BENEDICTION

On your feet! All pride aside, "put your whole self in" and fess up!

"Shake yourself about,"—rearrange your priorities, clear your vision.

Now you're ready, with God's help, to "turn yourself around," —to live in accordance with God's will and for God's glory, now and always, because, as the song declares, "That's what it's all about." (Clap!)

ABOUT THE AUTHOR

Rev. Dr. Janice Six

Born and reared in Abilene, Texas, Janice is a third-generation member of First Central Presbyterian Church (FCPC) where her grandparents joined in 1925. It was here that she was baptized and confirmed, married, and ordained as a deacon and elder before being ordained as Minister of Word and Sacrament of the Presbyterian Church (USA). Janice is the first female to be installed as a pastor at FCPC. Prior to being called as Associate Pastor, Janice served as Director of Christian Education for eight years. She retired in 2022 after 25 years of service.

Janice is married to Gene Six, and they have two children, Greg and Julia—both baptized and married at FCPC. Greg is married to Trudy, and Julia to Jace. Greg and Trudy's daughter, Greer Louise, is the first of the fifth generation to be a baptized member of FCPC. All live in Abilene and are active in the church family.

Janice has a Master of Divinity degree (M.Div.) from Abilene Christian University's Graduate School of Theology and a Doctor of Ministry degree (D.Min.) from Louisville Presbyterian Theological Seminary.

* 9 7 9 8 9 8 7 3 3 5 1 5 4 *